St. Louis STARS

NINE UNIQUE QUILTS THAT SPARK

by Toby Lischko

St. Louis Stars

By Toby Lischko

Edited by Judy Pearlstein

Tech edited by Jeri Brice

Design by Brian Grubb

Quilt Photographs by Aaron Leimkuehler

Illustrations by Toby Lischko

Production Assistance by Jo Ann Groves

Published by Kansas City Star Books
1729 GRAND BOULEVARD
KANSAS CITY, MISSOURI 64108

First edition, first printing
ISBN: 978-1-935362-06-7
Library of Congress Control Number 2009923432

Printed in the United States of America
By Walsworth Publishing Co.
Marceline, Missouri

To order copies, call StarInfo,
816-234-4636 (Say "Operator.")

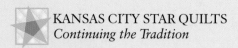

KANSAS CITY STAR QUILTS
Continuing the Tradition

The Quilter's Home Page

www.Pickledish.com
http://www.pickledish.com/
The Quilter's Home Page

Acknowledgements and Dedication

I would be remiss if I didn't thank all the people that have contributed to my accomplishments as a quilter: first and foremost, my husband Mike, who has for the most part, cheerfully accepted being a quilt widower when I spend so many hours in my sewing room and go on teaching and quilt show trips; my parents, who have always taught me to be the best at anything that I want to be and that I can do anything I put my mind to; and my friends and business associates (quilters and non-quilters) who constantly encourage me to obtain my goals. Thanks to my closest friends: Dolores, Terri, Sandi, Wanda, Hallye, Art, and Kathy, who have always encouraged me and shared in my thrill with success.

The national teachers who have taught me wonderful skills, including Sharyn Craig, whose techniques I constantly share with my own students. Marti Michell, whose templates are a wonderful contribution to the quilting world, who was willing to let me play with them for my own designs, and freely gave me advice regarding traveling and teaching.

The fabric companies who supply me with such wonderful fabrics: Julie Scribner of P&B Textiles who gave me my first chance to prove myself as a designer and Demetrius Zahoudanis and Beatriz Ordonez of RJR Fabrics who had faith in my ability to design for them. Emily Cohen, of Timeless Treasures, who always sends me beautiful fabrics to design with, and Sandy Muckenthaler of Hoffman Fabrics who has me designing virtual quilts and always loves my work.

The magazine editors who put me in print: Sue Harvey and Sandra Hatch of *Quilter's World* magazine who accepted my first and second article and lots of quilt patterns to help me on my way to national recognition. Beth Hayes of *McCall's Quilting*, Vivian Ritter of CK Media, Laurette Koserowski of *The Quilter* and Deb Hearn of *Quilt* who have always been kind and accepting of my designs. And of course, Doug Weaver, of Kansas City Star publications, who agreed to publish my first book, my editor, Judy Pearlstein, and my designer, Brian Grubb.

All of the quilters, whether internationally known or in my local guilds, were willing to share information and happiness. I have found that quilters are the most giving and sharing people in the world and none of them were afraid of a little competition. This book is dedicated to all of them.

The Quilts

Table of Contents

About the Author

Toby took her first quilting class in 1985, along with her mother, from the renowned Jackie Robinson, who owned the quilt shop in St. Louis. It was during summer vacation from her job as a Special Education teacher. After the six-week class she got the quilting bug. In 1995, she starting working in a quilt shop and began to teach quilting, design her own quilts, and enter contests. In 2005, she won a first place prize in the First Entry, Wall division for "her masterpiece," Celestial Crowns, featured in the AQS 2006 calendar. In 2007, she retired from education and began concentrating on her quilting career, setting some high goals, including teaching at a national venue and writing a book. In 2007 and 2008 she was asked to teach at the Houston Quilt Festival.

Photo by Faller Photography Group,
Edwardsville, Il.

An award winning quilter, pattern designer, and quilt teacher, she enjoys the whole process. "I love taking a group of fabrics and creating a unique design that shows off the collection." Her entries into the Hoffman Challenge in 1996 were accepted in the traveling shows and she won a second place prize in 1997 for the pieced division. Her skill and her unique style have been recognized by many of the major fabric companies, such as Timeless Treasures, Hoffman, and P&B, who regularly commission her to design quilts for them.

She considers herself a traditional quilter with a twist. "I use traditional blocks to create quilts that look difficult but that anyone can make." Her patterns and designs can be found in quilt shops, on the web, and in many of the national quilting magazines such as *McCall's Quilting*, *The Quilter*, and *Quilt*. She was featured in *Miniature Quilt Magazine* and wrote articles for *Quilter's World*.

She lives in the rural area of Robertsville, Missouri, with her husband of 36 years, Mike, a Marine Corp Vietnam veteran, and two dogs and five cats. They have two grown children, Rachel and Nicholas, a son-in-law Ed, and three grandchildren, Jeremy, Danielle, and Aiden. She runs her own business, Gateway Quilts & Stuff, Inc. and has a website, www.gatewayquiltsnstuff.com, where her patterns and workshop descriptions can be found. She hopes that many readers, from beginners to accomplished quilters, will enjoy this book, the first of many she plans.

*In memory of my dear mother-in-law,
Mary Lischko, who treated me like a
daughter and brightened everyone's day.*

Introduction

My fascination with the St. Louis Star block began in 1996 when a book called *Mirror Manipulations* by Gail Valentine came into the shop where I was working. I had used mirrors in other quilts I had made, but her book also introduced drafting 8-point stars of all kinds along with using mirrors to find unique designs. I was especially intrigued with the St. Louis Star block due to the different design possibilities. Maybe the name also drew me to it since I was born and raised in St. Louis. I made some quilts from the book to use as samples for classes and then designed my first commissioned quilt for P & B Textiles using it with a Courthouse Steps block. I named that quilt *St. Louis Courthouse Steps* (photo and pattern on beginning on page 42).

I started teaching drafting classes based on that book and on using mirrors to create wonderful quilts to show off the individuality of the students in the class. One of my students was so taken with the technique, that she made four more quilts after taking the class and used some of her "ugly" fabrics that she had in her stash. It was a block that no matter what kind of fabric you used in it, it still looked good. In 2000, I created *Stars Over St. Louis* for a state guild challenge (page 30). I combined the block with a LeMoyne Star block so that I could create other kaleidoscope designs. It won a first place prize from the guild challenge and also a machine quilting award from *Miniature Quilt* magazine and appeared in issues #65 and #68.

When I started designing for magazines, I created *Ornamental Stars* (p. 52) for *Quilt It For Christmas* 2005, published by CK Media. After that pattern came out, I decided to teach a class specifically on just the St. Louis Star and show how easily the block pieced together since it had no Y seams. With the help of Electric Quilt software, a popular quilt designing program, I no longer had to teach how to draft it, since the pattern for the templates could be printed out and reproduced. I concentrated instead on construction techniques. It became a popular class, which I was asked to teach at the International Quilt Association show in Houston in 2007 and 2008. Since it grew in popularity, I had my own acrylic templates made so that students did not have to spend as much time in class creating their own plastic templates.

This book is dedicated to all of those quilters that want to take that next step. The block is a little more challenging than the typical Ohio star, but easier than the LeMoyne star, and not so difficult that a beginning quilter cannot learn to make it. I give step-by-step directions to break it down so that anyone can be successful at it. There are templates at the back of the book and instructions for making your own templates, but also instructions on how you can order the acrylic templates for better accuracy. I have also included blank blocks (page 95) so that you can play with your own colorway and create blocks that are uniquely yours. Feel free to make copies of that page for your designing pleasure.

I want quilting to be fun. So have fun working with this book, creating your own blocks, and making quilts that you love to keep or give away.

I wanted to write this book to show off many of the wonderful design possibilities with this block. Playing on my EQ6, I realized that there are so many more combinations that I cannot fit into all of the pages of this book, but hope that once you start making some of the quilts in the following pages, it will encourage you to try your own designs with this block. I have included a page of blank stars that you may copy as many times as you wish so that you can create your own color combinations.

The most important thing I want you to come away with after reading this book and playing with this block is my basic philosophy, "Quilting should be fun"! You should always enjoy what you make and have fun sharing it with others. I certainly have.

How To Use This Book

I recommend that you read through "Getting Started" on page 8 and "Constructing the St. Louis Star Block" on page 18 to get an idea of what fabrics work best with this block and how the block is pieced before beginning any of the projects.

"Getting Started," beginning on page 8, introduces you to different types of fabrics that work well with the center of the block, plus how to put colors together for the best effect or to create the effect you want. It also shows how to make and use your own templates. In addition, there are templates available for purchase through my website, www.gatewayquiltsnstuff.com, for all of the different size St. Louis Star blocks in this book. Included are quilting tools that I personally use for better piecing, along with how to use mirrors to find repeats and the best way to cut out the eight repeats.

The second chapter, "Constructing the St. Louis Star Block, beginning on page 18, gives you step-by-step directions and piecing tips on how to construct the St. Louis Star block. A good suggestion is that you make a couple of test blocks before starting the quilts in this book. Practice makes perfect and you will find the block gets easier the more you piece it. Included is how to get a perfect 1/4" seam every time, which is extremely important for the block to be accurate. There are 32 pieces in this block (don't let that scare you) and for every seam that is not accurate, it affects the squareness of the block.

"The Quilts" chapter begins on page 24. An image of the St. Louis Star block used in each one is included. (Remember to use "Constructing the St. Louis Star Block" on page 18 for piecing this part of the quilt.) Some of the quilts have options for other sizes. Each pattern includes fabric suggestions.

Chapter 4 "Finishing," beginning on page 74, has basic quilt assembly, directions on construction of borders including mitering, bindings and options for piecing backs.

Chapter 5, beginning on page 82, is a gallery of quilts that I have made with the St. Louis Star block, quilt patterns in this book, along with some of my students' quilts and projects they have done with the block.

Chapter 6, contains the templates you'll need, and begins on page 90.

I've tried to make enough different kinds of quilts in this book so that anyone can find something that piques their interest. They range from simple four-block patterns to queen and king size quilts with reproduction, batik, oriental, and fantastic collections from many of the major fabric companies. So sit back, relax, and enjoy!

Getting Started

Getting Started

Choosing Fabrics

This is my favorite part of the design process. Once you start using mirrors to create different effects with blocks, you will never look at fabric in the same way. Whenever I walk into a quilt shop, I can't resist purchasing fabric that I know will make fantastic quilt blocks. There are a few basic things that I look for when making the St. Louis Star block.

HIGH CONTRAST

The first thing I look for is high contrast, both in the background and in the colors. Bright florals, oriental prints, and geometric designs are good examples.

Fabric 1 was used in my small *Stars Over St. Louis* quilt on page 29.

Fabric 2 was used in my large *Stars Over St. Louis* quilt (page 89).

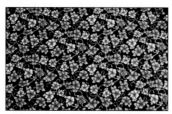

Fabric 3 was used in *St. Louis Courthouse Steps* (page 42).

Other examples of good high contrast fabrics:

Fabric 4

Fabric 5

Fabric 6

NUMBER OF REPEATS

Some fabrics have lots of wonderful repeats. Stripes are fantastic to play with, especially when there are a couple different types of stripes within the fabric to pick from. Fabric 7 was used in *Midnight in the Butterfly Garden* (page 48). It did not have a lot of different patterns in it, but the repetition effect I created by using the same place in each block gave the quilt stability and a look that I had not originally thought of. Fabric 8 is a stripe with a wonderful floral.

Fabric 7

Fabric 8

FABRIC COLLECTIONS

Fabric 9

I like to look at fabric collections because many times there are multiple colorways of the same pattern. Fabric 9 is an RJR Thimbleberries collection that had three different colorways of the same print. I was able to use the same place in each fabric for all of the blocks on the *Falling Stars* quilt (page 68). Fabric 10 has the same pattern with dark and light backgrounds. I like interchanging them to use in the center of the block.

Fabric 10

SYMMETRICAL VS. ASYMMETRICAL

Fabric patterns are either symmetrical or asymmetrical. Symmetrical means that the design element is the same on both sides of a center point. Fabric 11 and 12 are examples of symmetrical patterns.

Asymmetrical patterns are designs that have no symmetry (basically everything else). Paisley, florals, and juvenile or novelty prints are usually asymmetrical and fun to work with.

Fabric 11

Fabric 13

Fabric 12

Fabric 14

COORDINATING FABRICS

For the surrounding part of the block, you have to determine what kind of effect you want to create. As a general rule, I like to start with a theme fabric (can be the center of the block or the border fabric) and then choose a light or dark for the background, and two contrasting fabrics for the outer points.

Fabric placement is what creates the unique effects of this block. Take a look at the three blocks that make up the *Ornamental Stars* quilt, page 52. Each block looks very different and when you first see them you wouldn't think they were the same block.

Of course there are no rules for fabric placement in this block. In the back of this book are plain St. Louis Star blocks (page 95). Play with different color placements. Start with two colors and keep adding colors until you find a combination you like. One of the St. Louis Star blocks in this book has six different colors in it. (*Autumn in New England* on page 56)

Quilting Tools

There are some basic tools that I always use when getting ready to make the St. Louis star block. Creating the kaleidoscope design in the center of the block is optional, but does make the block more interesting.

1. Templates – Heavy clear template plastic is preferable. Purchased acrylic templates are available in a variety of sizes, 8 1/2", 10", 12", and 17" on my website www.gatewayquiltsnstuff.com, or you can ask your local quilt shop to carry them.

2. Scotch tape, the cheaper the better.

3. Small rotary cutter, 18 mm is best for smaller blocks, especially when fussy-cutting, so you do not cut into designs you might want to use. The 28 mm is good too — any larger than that makes it difficult to control.

4. Dr. Scholl's Molefoam Pad for establishing an exact 1/4".

5. Collins seam gauge with reference holes.

6. Silk pins, .5 mm or smaller. Don't be fooled by a package that states "silk pins." Be sure to look at the width of the pin.

7. Thread — my favorite piecing thread is Superior Masterpiece thread designed by Alex Anderson. It is a 50 wt. long staple 100% cotton thread.

8. Marti Michell's Magic Mirrors.

9. Fork pins - these are wonderful for matching points when piecing. They are two pins in one.

How to Use the Mirrors

To set the mirrors at the angle you need for the center, place the template A or E (narrow end), inside the mirror and lay a piece of tape across the top to set it. It doesn't make any difference which size template A or E you use to create the angle, the angle remains the same on all sizes.

If you want to see what the center will look like pieced, place the mirror inside the seam lines on the template. With a symmetrical design, what you see in the mirror is what you will get.

Setting mirror at proper angle

Symmetrical Fabric

Image in mirror

Resulting center

If you place the mirror on either side of the same symmetrical fabric you will see a left and right image (mirror image). If you choose this option you will have to cut out a left and right piece. To do this you will turn the template upside down for the opposite piece.

Image in mirror

Resulting center

Floral in mirror   Resulting center design

For floral or asymmetrical prints, the mirror will give me a basic effect of what it might look like, but what you see in the mirror is not exactly what you will get because the left and right sides of the design usually are not exactly the same.

In this design, when you look at it in the mirror, you see a yellow center that is reflected on the left side of the mirror. When you look at the center of the block laid out, the yellow curves to the left in each section.

A better example of this is with this dog fabric. When you place the mirror on one of the dogs you will see a ball to the right of the dog and you see the reflection in the mirror. When you put the center of the block together, the ball goes around on the right side in each section.

Dog in mirror   Resulting center design

I like to play with the mirror by moving it around the fabric to get an idea of how many different designs I can find before cutting them out. That way I can see if one of my designs will cut into another that I like.

To Fussy-Cut or Not to Fussy-Cut

Center not fussy-cut

When I find a fabric I want to use in this block, I find I do not always need to fussy-cut the center. Of course you will not need to fussy-cut it if you are using batiks or very small prints; however, sometimes I think I don't need to fussy-cut it but find out after making a sample block that it looks better when I do. Take for example the *Falling Stars* quilt (page 68). I cut out the center template without regards to the design of the fabric and got the following results (see left).

Center fussy-cut

I then thought, "what would it look like if I did decide to fussy-cut it," and got the following results:

I certainly liked the second results better and went ahead and cut the rest of the blocks in the same manner. You don't have to put the whole block together to see what it would look like. Of course the block will look slightly different once the seams are sewn, but you can get the general idea by placing them next to each other on your design board.

How Much Fabric Do I Need?

When purchasing fabric for one of these projects you will need to take a couple things into account.

Scale: I have to admit, I don't think about scale when I purchase a fabric I want to use in this block. I just buy it because I like it. But I do have to think about it when I decide which project I want to use it in.

For the 8 1/2" and 10" blocks I look for small prints. The small floral that I used in the *St. Louis Courthouse Steps* quilt (page 42) is a good example of a small print. The flowers were slightly different so that I could create different centers in each of the blocks.

Small floral

Sometimes the fabric has small motifs that can be used in the center of the block, but not necessarily as a repetition. The Laurel Burch print that I used in the center of the *Cats in Stars* quilt (in the gallery on page 88) is a good example of this. Because there were a lot of different cats to choose from, I did not feel that there had to be a kaleidoscope effect in the middle and I cut out different cats for each of the sections. THERE ARE NO RULES! Do what makes you happy. For the 12" block you can use a small to medium size print and for the 17" block you can use a medium to large print.

Laurel Burch cat print

To determine whether the scale will work with the size block I want to use, I use my template to see what part of the pattern fits within the seam lines. If the motif takes up the whole space, you lose the repetition effect.

Number of repeats: You have to look at the fabric to see how close together the repeats are, both across the selvage grain and the width of the fabric. Some prints can have repeats as close as 6" or smaller across the width and then repeat again halfway in between those in the next row. With repeats this close, depending on the size of the block, you may not be able to cut a lot of different areas around your original cut.

Print used in Autumn in New England

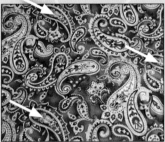

Paisley fabric

On other fabrics, the repeats may be farther apart, but you will be able to use more of the open areas for cutting a variety of different motifs.

With symmetrical prints or stripes it is a lot easier to imagine how many different prints you can get from them since you are going along a straight line.

Since this block has eight repeats in it, figure out how many repeats you can get from one yard of fabric and go from there. Many times when I find a fabric I like and I'm not sure what project I will be using it in, I will purchase twice the yardage I think I will need. I learned my lesson while making one of my competition quilts as I was running out of fabric and had to do a desperate search for more of it! That's not easy when the fabric is 3 years old.

Don't disregard prints that you may not think can create a kaleidoscope effect in the center. I have had this swirl fabric for quite some time and I decided to experiment with it to see what I could come up with. I was pleasantly surprised at the wonderful blocks it created (Psychedelic Stars quilt in page 64). In order to make certain elements of the swirl (specific colors) really pop out, I used a fabric in the points to bring out those colors.

Swirl fabric

I do suggest that if you have never done any fussy-cutting before, that you start with a design that does not have to match on the sides of the center patches. Symmetrical designs require more matching and more accurate piecing in the center. Either choose a fabric that has large spaces between the designs like the cat fabric or floral and busy fabrics that will create a unique design no matter where you cut them.

Using the Templates

I find that the easiest way to make the templates, if you have not purchased them, is to first copy the template page on a copier. Then cut out the pieces and tape them to the template plastic with some rolled up tape on the back of the paper. Cut them both out cutting off the line at the same time. I find that process much easier than trying to trace the template. It is very important to be as accurate as you can, because the accuracy of your templates will give you the best results when piecing the block. Take off the paper and label your templates with the letter, size, and type of block it creates. I also write down what size strip to cut for each template. Remember, cut out a slightly larger strip than is needed.

After you find the design you want to cut out, place a couple pieces of rolled up tape on the back of the template and cut out your first piece of fabric. If I'm using template plastic, I like to use the 18 mm rotary cutter. It will not cut into areas that I may want to use in another repeat, plus I have better control of it to keep it from cutting into my template. If I am using purchased acrylic templates, the 18 mm or 28 mm rotary cutter works as well. If you use the larger rotary cutters, you have less control. Leave that fabric on the template because you will use it to find the next seven repeats. Simply find the area of the repeat, place the template with the fabric on it onto the repeat until it disappears into the fabric. Cut it out and repeat until you have all eight pieces. Do not take off your original piece. Go to the next area and repeat the process until you have all of the sections cut out that you need.

In the cutting instructions for the coordinating fabrics, I purposely have you cut the strips slightly larger than the template. This way if the edges are not perfectly aligned you have a little extra room to center the template to be sure that the top and bottom fabrics completely cover it. Be sure to trim off the corners to make piecing easier. Pay attention to the grain line. Some triangles you will cut with the grain line along the long edge and some along the short edge. I do not cut more than two layers at a time. The more layers you cut the more you reduce the accuracy of your cutting. Each quilt cutting instructions will include which sides you will need to place together before cutting B/Br. This will create your left and right sides of the points of the star and eliminates the need to turn the template upside-down for the reverse side. For all blocks, you will need 8 A, 8 B, 8 Br, 4 C, and 4 D.

Now you are ready for the next chapter:
St. Louis Star block construction.

B/Br cutting placement

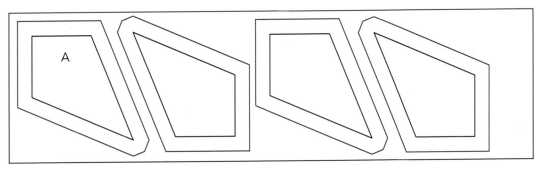

A cutting placement if not fussy-cutting

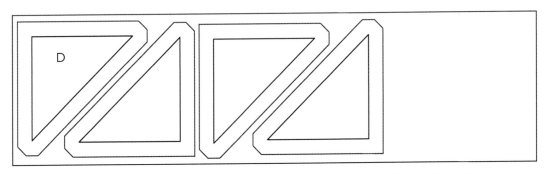

D cutting placement short edge straight-of-grain

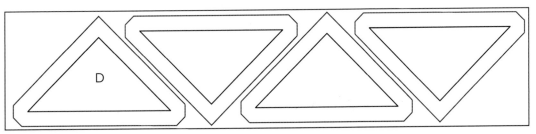

D cutting placement long edge straight-of-grain

Constructing the St. Louis Star Block

Piecing tips

The number one priority of any piecing is an accurate 1/4" seam allowance. I don't like using a "scant 1/4" because everyone's definition of it is different. By using an accurate 1/4", everyone is sewing at the same place. Try this for an accurate 1/4" seam. Put the needle in the farthest right position as possible on your machine. With the Collins Seam Gauge, place your needle in the 1/4" hole or measure an exact 1/4" from the needle using one of your rotary rulers. Use a small strip of Dr. Scholl's Molefoam padding next to your machine foot at this measurement. (You can get this at any drug store.) If you cannot move your needle, place a small piece of the molefoam in front and behind the foot. I cut the molefoam 1/4" wide with my rotary cutter and then into small 3/8" or 1/2" pieces. You can see with my needle in this position, I can always see if my fabric is lined up with the 1/4" guide. To test your 1/4" seam, cut three small strips at 1 1/2" each and sew them together. The center strip should measure 1" exactly. Adjust your molefoam accordingly. I test my 1/4" every time I sit down to sew so I know my seams will be accurate.

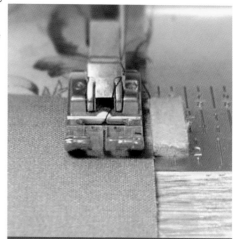

Molefoam placed 1/4" from needle

Three important things to consider

I have found, when teaching this block or any other class, that there are three reasons most people have difficulty with the block coming out SQUARE and with points or edges without 1/4" allowances. These are things that I look at when people bring their blocks to me to find out why they don't look right.

THE FIRST REASON IS:

The templates are not cut out accurately. There are times when the fabric on the bottom (or top) moves and you don't realize it. That is the first thing that I check when pieces do not match. I will line them up with the template to see if they are cut too small or too big and either make an adjustment or cut out a new piece. This is also true for strips, SQUARES, or any other shape you may cut for your projects. Always check to make sure that your cutting is accurate.

THE SECOND REASON IS:

You do not have a consistent 1/4" seam. Consistency is the key! Using the molefoam, I always have a consistent 1/4" seam from the beginning to the end of my sewing edge. Always check your seams for accuracy. The best way to do this is after you have completed the different sections of the block. Each of the sections should be exactly the same size. By stacking them on top of each other, I can check to see if they are the same. It is easier to fix as I go when I do this, than to wait until the complete block is put together.

THE THIRD AND FINAL REASON IS:

The edges of the two fabrics are not aligned. You would be surprised to know that even if you are off 1/16th or 1/32nd of an inch that it can throw off the entire block! With 32 pieces in this block, each fraction of an inch changes the block's alignment. Check your edges often and lift them up to check underneath as you sew, to make sure they are even.

TAKE YOUR TIME WHEN SEWING. I always tell my students, "This is not a race." If you take your time, your accuracy increases and you will do less "unsewing"! Also, let the machine do the work for you. Do not push or pull your fabric as it is being sewn, especially since this block has many bias edges.

Cutting tips

For template B and Br (the reverse of B), cut them out at the same time. For some quilts you will place fabric #1 on top, wrong sides together with fabric #2 and only cut with template B right side up. Br will be cut at the same time on the bottom fabric. Sometimes you will have fabric #2 on top. For other quilts you will fold one fabric strip in half, wrong sides together, and cut B and Br out at the same time. You may at times, place both strips of the fabric right side up or right side down depending on whether you are cutting B or Br. Pay attention to each quilt pattern as it will give you specific directions on how to cut out B/Br.

When cutting the template D, for most of the quilts the grain line is along the long edge of the triangle. Pay attention to which direction to place the template because some blocks may have you cutting the same template with two different grain line placements. (Templates begin on page 90.)

Pressing tips

Pay attention to pressing directions. They will help the block fit together better. Some seams are pressed open for less bulk. I finger-press my seams first from the front when they are pressed to one side and from the back when they are pressed open. This assures me that my seams are completely flat before I add heat. Then I press on the side that I finger-pressed first and turn it over and press on the opposite side. There are a lot of bias edges in this block, especially if you fussy cut the inside section. A dry iron keeps the block from getting distorted with steam. When you finish the entire block, spray it with starch or water and press with an up and down action, not side to side. This will flatten the block out nicely and set the seams. If you do find that your block is slightly smaller or larger than the finished block should be, you can trim or block it if necessary; however, do not trim too much and lose the 1/4" seam at the points. I don't usually trim my blocks if I find that they are all pretty close to the same size, even if they are slightly larger or smaller. The surrounding blocks or sections will help regulate the block size, and quilting it will hide any inconsistencies if they are not too blatant.

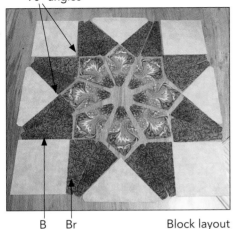

90° angles

B   Br   Block layout

General Piecing Instructions

Start out by laying out the complete block to the left of your sewing machine following this illustration. After each step, you will be referred back to this diagram. The first time you lay this out, it may take you a while to get B and Br in the right direction. You will know if you have it right when you pay attention to the 90° angle which should be aligned with the 90° angle on the square or triangle. So I don't get confused, I will lay out all of the B sections and Br sections together and then place them in the block where they belong.

This block is constructed in eighths.

Important: Sew in the direction of the arrows for all piecing..
Tip: To check for accuracy, stack each section or group as you get them done to make sure they are all the same size. **Correct mistakes as you go.**

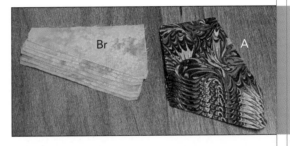

Stack

Step 1.
UNIT 1.

Pick up all A sections and stack them. Pick up all Br sections and stack them to the left of A as shown. With right sides together, sew A to Br chain style, one right after the other. Clip apart. Press to A. Place these back in the same place on your block.

Tip: I always sew from the 90° angle (direction of the arrows) to make sure that the edges are even.

Sew. Press to A.

Step 2.
UNIT 2.

Pick up all C squares and stack them. Pick up 4 B sections and stack them to the right of C. Sew B to C chain style, one right after the other. Press to C. Clip apart. Place these back in the same place on your block.

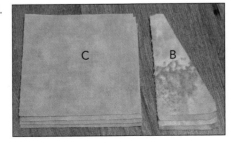

Stack

Sew. Press to C.
You will have to turn patches over to sew in the direction of the arrow.

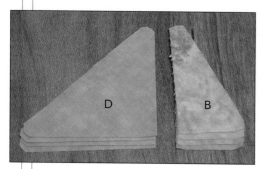

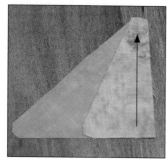

Stack   Sew. Press to D.

Step 3.
UNIT 3.
Pick up all D triangles and stack them. Pick up the remaining 4 B sections and stack them to the right of D. Sew D to B chain style. Press to D. Place these back in the same place on your block.

Step 4.
GROUP 1.
Pick up and stack four of Unit 1. Pick up and stack all of Unit 2 to the left of Unit 1 as illustrated. Place right sides together, match seams, pin, and sew (in direction of arrow).

Tip: Always pin just in front of the seam. Press to Unit 2. Place them back in the block.

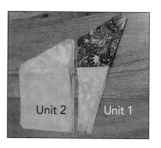

Stack   Sew. Press to Unit 2.

Stack   Sew Press to Unit 3

Step 5.
GROUP 2.
Pick up and stack the remaining Unit 1. Pick up and stack all of Unit 3 to the left of Unit 1. Match seams, pin, and sew. Press to Unit 3. Place them back in the block.

You have now created the eight sections of the block
(four Group 1 and four Group 2). Each one of these sections should be the same size. This is a good time to check the accuracy of your piecing, by placing the same groups on top of each other, to fix any problems before they become too difficult to fix.

Step 6.
Stack all of Group 1 and all of Group 2. (Photos top of p. 23.) Place them next to each other. Group 2 should always be to the right of Group 1. (You find out very quickly what happens when you have them on the wrong sides!) Match seams, pin, and sew. The two seams from each group should be lined up directly on top of each other *(detail 1)*. Sew from the inside of the seam to the outside, placing the pin at the outside edge parallel to the seam line and weaving it in and out *(detail 2)*. Pull the pin out slowly as you sew to the outside edge. This will keep the edges together as you sew. Take your time sewing this seam and make sure that you keep a consistent 1/4" all the way to the top.

Tip: The bulk of the two seams have a tendency to push away from the molefoam, so I stop frequently with my needle down and reposition the edge. Press seams open. You now have four quarters finished.

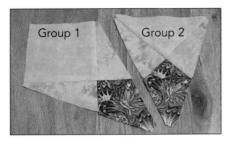

Stack (top)

Sew units 1 and 2 together. Press seams open (left).

Step 7. Sew the quarters together, creating two halves, matching seams and pinning edges as shown to the right.. Press seams open.

Detail 1 Overlap seams

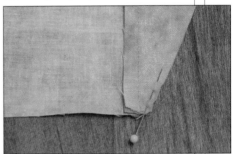

Detail 2 Pinning

Sew quarters together. Press seam open.

Step 8. Sew the halves together. Match the center seams and place a pin on each side of the center seam (or use a forked pin). Repeat the pinning technique for the outside edge of the block. Sew from the center seam to the outside edge. Turn block over and repeat for the other half of the seam. Press seam open.

Sew halves together. Press seam open.

I like to do a couple of practice blocks first. I can then make any corrections to my piecing if needed, so that the block comes out at the size I want. That way I don't use my good fabric before I'm ready.

READY FOR THE QUILTS? See individual quilt instructions starting on page 24. Refer back to general piecing instructions for the St. Louis Star block beginning on page 21.

You will follow these instructions for all of the St. Louis Star blocks in the book. They will not be repeated for every pattern. You will need to follow the cutting instructions carefully for fabric placement.

Back view

Reproduction Stars

I've been collecting reproduction fabrics for a long time. They make wonderful baby quilts. I designed this quilt so that it would be fat quarter friendly. You can create this quilt with twelve fat quarters and a background fabric. I chose two of each fabric color for each block and muslin for the background. For variety you could interchange the colors in each block or use twelve different colors. You can also use juvenile prints or tone-on-tones.

QUILT INFORMATION

Quilt size: 39" x 54"

Block size: 12"

Number of blocks: 6

Block layout: Straight set with sash and nine-patch cornerstones.

Template size 12" on page 91

FABRIC REQUIREMENTS

Small print such as reproduction fabrics for blocks, sashing, borders, and binding	12 fat quarters (2 each color)
Background	1 1/2 yards
Backing	1 3/4 yards
Batting	45" x 65"

Cutting Instructions

All strips are cut width of fabric (WOF).

Cut B/Br with the two same colored fabrics placed wrong sides together.
*Cut the larger pieces (binding, border, sashing) from the fat quarters first, before cutting the other pieces. Cut along the long edge (20" side).

Reproduction Stars
By Toby Lischko, 2008, Quilted by Terri Kanyuck, Labadie, Mo.
Baby/lap size, 39" x 54"
Fabrics by Windham, Storybook V collection.

Who doesn't like a baby quilt of reproduction fabrics? Using nine-patches in the sash and border make it look very traditional and irresistible! This is a fun quilt to put together using the fat quarters you have in your collection. Make the whole quilt top (and binding) with twelve fat quarters and muslin. Terri quilted flowers in the background and followed the center of the star to create a flower in the middle.

FABRIC	NUMBER OF STRIPS	SUB-CUT
Fat quarter (FQ) St. Louis Star blocks	(1) 4 1/8" strips from each FQ	8 B from one FQ and 8 Br from the other FQ of the same color
		(4) 1 1/2" x 12 1/2" each from 6 different color FQs
*Sashing		(1) 1 1/2" x 12 1/2" from 10 FQs
		(8) 1 1/2" x 1 1/2" from each FQ
Nine-patches		(8) 1 1/2" x 1 1/2" from each FQ plus (4) more from two of the FQs for a total of 104 squares
*Border		(1) 3 1/2" x 10 1/4" from 8 FQs
*Binding		(1) 2 1/4" x 20" from 10 FQs
Background St. Louis Star blocks	(8) 3 1/8" (3) 4 1/8"	48 A and 24 D 24 C
Sashing	(6) 1 1/2"	(17) 1 1/2" x 12 1/2"
Nine-patches	(5) 1 1/2"	(130) 1 1/2" x 1 1/2"

Block Construction

Read all instructions before piecing.

St. Louis Star blocks

Construct six blocks with each of the colors (2 of the same B/Br color in each block) following the general piecing instructions starting on page 21.

Sashing and nine-patches

I chose to "frame" the block with the same color 1 1/2" x 12 1/2" sashing strips (see quilt photo, page 24). Before sewing the strips into the sashing, lay out the blocks, sashing strips and nine-patches for a placement that you like.

NINE-PATCHES

1. Sew four 1 1/2" squares of a fat quarter color to five 1 1/2" squares background as illustrated to create a nine-patch. Press in the direction of the arrows. Make 26 nine-patches.

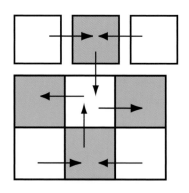

Create nine-patches
Press in direction of
arrows

SASHING SECTIONS

2. After determining where you want the colors of the sashing strips, sew two color 1 1/2" x 12 1/2" strips to one 1 1/2" x 12 1/2" background strip as illustrated. Press to color strips. Make 17 sections.

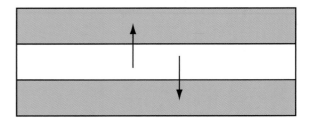

Create sashing sections
Press in direction of arrows

Quilt Construction

Following quilt layout, sew the stars, nine-patches and sashing sets together. Press to sashing strips.

Border Construction

1. Sew three nine-patches to four color 3 1/2" x 10 1/4" strips. Press to rectangles. Repeat. Sew onto the sides.

2. Sew four nine-patches to three color 3 1/2" x 9 1/2" strips. Press to rectangles. Repeat. Sew onto the top and bottom.

Follow finishing techniques beginning on page 74 in for layering, basting, quilting, and binding.

Stars Over St. Louis
Made and quilted by
Toby Lischko, 2002
Small wall size,
18" x 18"

I created this quilt for my state guild challenge. The theme of it was
stars. I wanted to continue the kaleidoscope effect in the corners so
I added LeMoyne Star blocks. The pieced ribbon-like border pulls it
together. All of the LeMoyne Stars and St. Louis Star block use the same
border fabric in them. It won first place at the guild retreat and also won
a machine quilting award in *Miniature Quilting Magazine*.

A fun quilt to try out those novelty or unusual prints that you weren't sure what to do with. Make a small quilt 18" x 18" or a larger quilt 36" x 36". I like to start with a wonderful print for the border and fussy-cut it for the center St. Louis Star and LeMoyne Star blocks. Choose a small print for the smaller quilt with a repeat no larger than 6" apart. Place template A and E on the print to see if the scale is appropriate for the size of the block. The larger quilt can have a repeat 6" to 12" apart. The ribbon border effect is easily pieced with rectangles and squares.

QUILT INFORMATION

Quilt size	18" x 18"	36" x 36"
St. Louis Star block	8 1/2"	17"
LeMoyne Star block	6"	12"

Template size for 18" quilt on page 94, A – H

Template size for 36" quilt on pages 92 – 93, A – H

FABRIC REQUIREMENTS (YARDS)

Quilt size	18" x 18"	36" x 36"
Theme fabric– Border #1, Border #2, template A and E	3/4 yard	1 1/2 yard
Background	1/4 yard	3/4 yard
Contrasting fabric #1 (red)		
Used in center block and border #1	1/8 yard	5/8 yard
Contrasting fabric #2 (blue)		
Used in center block, border #1 and binding	1/4 yard	3/4 yard
Back	21" square	40" square
Batting	21" square	40" square

Cutting Instructions

All strips are cut width of fabric (WOF).

Pay attention to the grain line on Template G and H when cutting triangles for the LeMoyne stars. Place fabrics #1 and #2 wrong sides together when cutting Template B/Br. Make sure fabric #1 is on top and template is right side up.

Tip: Because triangles G and H are the same size, but cut in different directions, place them in a baggie and label them.

Cutting Instructions *continued*

Quilt size	18" x 18"	36" x 36"
Theme print		
Template A	8 repeats	8 repeats
Template E	4 matching sets of 4 different repeats	4 matching sets of 4 different repeats
Border #1	Cut (8) 1 1/2" x 2 1/2" Cut (12) 1 1/2" square	Cut (8) 2 1/2" x 4 1/2" Cut (12) 2 1/2 " square
Border #2	Cut (4) 2 1/2" x 21" strips	Cut (4) 4 1/2" strips
Background		
Template C	Cut 4	Cut 4
Template D	Cut 4	Cut 4
Template F	Cut 4	Cut 4
Template G	Cut 8	Cut 8
Template H	Cut 8	Cut 8
Border #1	Cut (12) 1 1/2" x 2 1/2"	Cut (12) 2 1/2" x 4 1/2"
Fabric #1		
Template B	Cut 8	Cut 8
Border #1	Cut (12) 1 1/2" x 2 1/2	Cut (12) 2 1/2" x 4 1/2"
Fabric #2		
Template Br	Cut 8	Cut 8
Border #1	Cut (12) 1 1/2 x 2 1/2"	Cut (12) 2 1/2" x 4 1/2"
Binding	Cut (2) 1 1/8" strips	Cut (4) 2" strips

Block Construction

Read all instructions before piecing.

Construct one St. Louis Star block according to the general piecing instructions on page 21.

LEMOYNE STAR BLOCK
(make 4 half-blocks)

1. Lay out the four blocks as in diagram #1 with the four matching designs in each E and background fabrics of square F and triangles G and H. Make sure that the E sections are facing in the same direction.

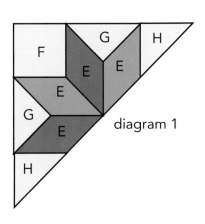

diagram 1

2. Sew two sections with two E and one G for each half-star block in the following manner:

diagram 2

3. With left E on the bottom and G on top, right sides together, sew from edge to edge as in diagram #3. Press to diamond E.

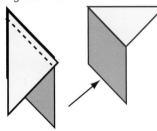

diagram 3

4. Place right diamond E right sides together on triangle G as in diagram #4. Sew from seam line (backstitch) to outside.

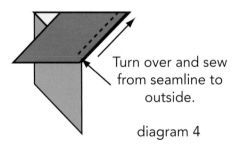

Turn over and sew from seamline to outside.

diagram 4

5. Fold so that the E diamonds are right sides together with triangle folded in half, as in diagram #4. Starting at the seam line from the triangle G (backstitch) and sew to the center of the block. Press open.

Fold triangle in half and diamonds right sides together. Sew from seam to center.

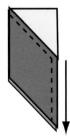

diagram 5

6. Repeat steps 3 through 5 for other two diamonds E and triangle G.

7. Place the F square between the two sections. Pick up left section and place the square right sides together on the diamond. Sew from edge to edge as in diagram #6.

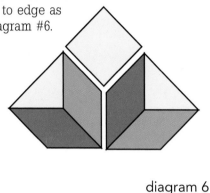

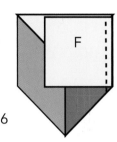

diagram 6

8. Repeat remaining two sides as in steps 4 and 5 with the square and the remaining diamond section. Press seam to the square and the seam between the diamonds open.

9. Sew triangle H to each end of the section. Press to diamonds. Repeat for remaining three half-LeMoyne stars.

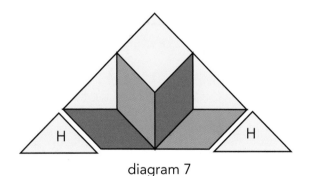

diagram 7

Quilt Center Construction

10. Sew a half-LeMoyne star section to each side of the center star, matching center and edges. Press away from the center star.

Border Construction

Instructions for the 36" quilt are in parentheses

11. Place a 1 1/2" x 2 1/2" (2 1/2" x 4 1/2") fabric #1 on the left end of a 1 1/2" x 2 1/2" (2 1/2" x 4 1/2") background (b) (rectangle, right sides together as shown. Draw a 45° line from the corner as shown. Stitch along the line. Trim the seam allowance to 1/4". Press to fabric #1.

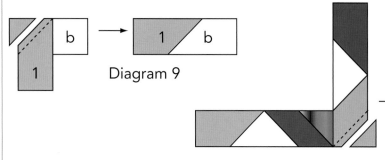

Diagram 9

12. Place a 1 1/2" x 2 1/2" (2 1/2" x 4 1/2") fabric #2 rectangle on the right end of the b rectangle, right sides together. Draw a 45° line from the corner as shown. Stitch along the line. Press towards fabric #2. Trim seam allowance. This completes Unit 1. Make a total of six of Unit 1.

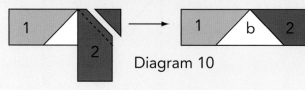

Diagram 10

13. Repeat steps 11 and 12 and make six Unit 2, starting with fabric #2 on the left and fabric #1 on the right.

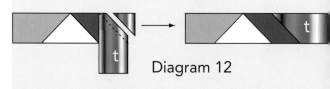

Diagram 11

14. Starting with Unit 1, place a 1 1/2" x 2 1/2" (2 1/2" x 4 1/2") theme (t) rectangle on fabric #2, right side together. Draw a 45° line from the corner as shown. Stitch along the line. Press seam toward fabric #2. Trim seam.

Diagram 12

15. Place the fabric #1 end of Unit 1 on the end of the theme fabric right sides together as shown. Draw a 45° line from the corner as shown. Stitch along the line. Press to fabric #1. Trim.

Diagram 13

16. Repeat steps 14 and 15. Border will look like diagram #14. Make one more border like this for Border 1a.

Diagram 14

17. Repeat steps 14 through 16 using unit 2 switching fabric #1 for #2 and #2 for #1. Border 1b will look like this:

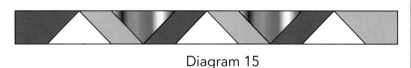

Diagram 15

18. Draw a diagonal line on the backs of the 1 1/2" (2 1/2") theme fabric squares. Sew to each end of all border units as shown. Stitch from corner to corner. Press to triangles and trim.

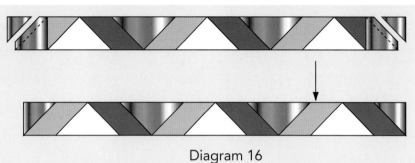

Diagram 16

19. Sew a 1 1/2" (2 1/2") theme square to each end of borders 1a.

Following the quilt layout, sew the 1b side borders on. Then add 1a top and bottom borders. Sew on border #2 following border techniques beginning on page 77.

Layering, basting, quilting, and binding instructions are on page 80. For the smaller quilt do not fold binding strip in half. Sew one edge of the binding strip, right sides together to the quilt top in the same way as the double fold binding. Fold binding over to the back, turn under 1/4" and hand-sew to the back of the quilt.

Stars Over St. Louis quilt layout

Here's To the Red, White, and Blue

I love working with batiks and had to make at least one St. Louis Star quilt with them. These batiks are a wonderful collection of Hoffman's 1895 batiks. You can also use tone-on-tones, or almost solids. I wouldn't use busy prints unless they read as an almost solid. I chose red, white, and blue, but you can pick two contrasting colors and a light or dark background. Then, find four shades of each contrasting color in medium light, medium, medium dark, and dark. Don't be intimidated by the cutting. Start with the wall size quilt, which is done in holiday colors. This quilt will impress your friends! To keep pieces organized, place each group in a labeled baggie.

QUILT INFORMATION

Quilt size	King	Queen/Double	Twin	Wall
Finished size:	111" x 111"	90" x 100"	74" x 94"	53" x 53"
Number of blocks	81 total	56 total	48 total	16 total
Block size: 10"	40 St. Louis Star (20 A, 20 B)	28 St. Louis Star (14 A, 14 B)	24 St. Louis Star (12 A, 12 B)	8 St. Louis Star (4 A, 4 B)
	41 Log Cabin	28 Log Cabin	24 Log Cabin	8 Log Cabin
Block layout	9 x 9	7 x 8	6 x 8	4 x 4
Template size 10" on p. 90				

FABRIC REQUIREMENTS

	King	Queen/Dbl	Twin	Wall
Light - Both blocks Border #1	2 3/4 yards	2 yards	1 3/4 yards	7/8 yard
Med. lt. #1 (blue) Log Cabin	1/2 yard	1/3 yard	1/3 yard	1/4 yard
Med. lt. #2 (red) Log Cabin	1/2 yard	3/8 yard	1/3 yard	1/4 yard
Med. #1 Both blocks	1 1/2 yards	1 1/8 yards	1 yard	1/2 yard
Med. #2 Both blocks	1 3/4 yards	1 1/4 yards	1 yard	1/2 yard
Med. dk. #1 Both block	1 3/4 yards	1 1/4 yards	1 1/8 yards	1/2 yard
Med. dk. #2 Both blocks Border #2	2 3/4 yards	2 yards	1 5/8 yards	1 1/4 yards
Dark #1 Both blocks Border #3 & Binding	4 5/8 yards	3 3/4 yards	2 7/8 yards	1 5/8 yards
Dark #2, Both blocks	1 5/8 yards	1 1/4 yards	1 yard	1/2 yard
Back	10 yards	8 1/4 yards	6 7/8 yards	3 1/2 yards
Batting	King size	Queen size	Twin size	58" x 58"

Here's to the Red, White, and Blue
Made by Toby Lischko, 2008, Quilted by Terri Kanyuck, Labadie, Mo.
Twin size, 75" x 95"
Fabrics courtesy of Hoffman of California Fabric Company.

A wonderful quilt for showing off batiks. The alternating colored stars create a cascading effect and the log cabins make them look like they are flying across the quilt. Terri did a beautiful job quilting feathers across the logs.

Cutting Instructions

All strips are cut width of fabric (WOF).

Place fabrics #1 and #2 wrong sides together when cutting Template B/Br. Make sure fabric #1 is on top and template is right side up. Cut B/Br with same fabric folded wrong sides together. Cut larger log sections first from strips.

Fabric	King	Queen/Double	Twin	Wall
Light				
Log Cabin Block	3 sub-cut	2 sub-cut	2 sub-cut	1 sub-cut
2 1/8" strips	41	28	24	8
2 1/8" x 2 1/8"				
St. Louis Star	8 sub-cut	6 sub-cut	5 sub-cut	2 sub-cut
3 1/2" strips	80 C	56 C	48 C	16 C
2 3/4" strips	13 sub-cut	9 sub-cut	8 sub-cut	3 sub-cut
	160 D	112 D	96 D	32 D
Border #1 strips	10 – 2"	8 – 2"	8 – 1 1/2"	5 – 1 1/2"
Med. light #1 (blue)				
Log Cabin block				
1 3/8" strips	9 sub-cut	6 sub-cut	5 sub-cut	2 sub-cut
1 3/8" x 3 3/8"	41	28	24	8
1 3/8 x 4 1/4"	41	28	24	8
Med. light #2 (red)				
Log Cabin block				
1 3/4" strips	6 sub-cut	5 sub-cut	4 sub-cut	2 sub-cut
1 3/4" x 2 1/8"	41	28	24	8
1 3/4" x 3 3/8"	41	28	24	8
Med. #1				
Log Cabin block				
1 3/8" strips	13 sub-cut	9 sub-cut	8 sub-cut	3 sub-cut
1 3/8" x 5 1/2"	41	28	24	8
1 3/8" x 6 3/8"	41	28	24	8
St. Louis Star block				
2 5/8" strips	5 sub-cut	4 sub-cut	3 sub-cut	1 sub-cut
	80A	56A	48A	16A
3 1/2" strips	5 sub-cut	4 sub-cut	3 sub-cut	1 sub-cut
	80 B/80 Br	56 B/56 Br	48 B/48 Br	16 B/ 16 Br
Med. #2				
Log Cabin block				
1 3/4" strips	11 sub-cut	8 sub-cut	6 sub-cut	2 sub-cut
1 3/4" x 4 1/4"	41	28	24	8
1 3/4" x 5 1/2"	41	28	24	8

Fabric	King	Queen/Double	Twin	Wall
Med. #2				
St. Louis Star block				
2 5/8" strips	5 sub-cut	4 sub-cut	3 sub-cut	1 sub-cut
	80A	56A	48A	16A
3 1/2" strips	5 sub-cut	4 sub-cut	3 sub-cut	1 sub-cut
	80 B/80 Br	56 B/56 Br	48 B/48 Br	16 B/16 Br
Med. dark #1				
Log Cabin block				
1 3/8" strips	20 sub-cut	13 sub-cut	11 sub-cut	4 sub-cut
1 3/8" x 7 5/8"	41	28	24	8
1 3/8" x 8 1/2"	41	28	24	8
St. Louis Star block				
2 5/8" strips	5 sub-cut	4 sub-cut	3 sub-cut	1 sub-cut
	80A	56A	48A	16A
3 1/2" strips	4 sub-cut	3 sub-cut	3 sub-cut	1 sub-cut
	80 B/80 Br	56 B/56 Br	48 B/48 Br	16 B/16 Br
Med. dark #2				
Log Cabin Block				
1 3/4" strips	15 sub-cut	11 sub-cut	9 sub-cut	3 sub-cut
1 3/4" x 6 3/8"	41	28	24	8
1 3/4" x 7 5/8"	41	28	24	8
St. Louis Star block				
2 5/8" strips	5 sub-cut	4 sub-cut	3 sub-cut	1 sub-cut
	80A	56A	48A	16A
3 1/2" strips	5 sub-cut	4 sub-cut	3 sub-cut	1 sub-cut
	80 B/80 Br	56 B/56 Br	48 B/48 Br	16B/16 Br
Border #2 strips	10 – 3 1/2"	8 – 3"	8 – 2"	5 – 1 1/2"
Dark #1				
Log Cabin block				
1 3/8" strips	25 sub-cut	17 sub-cut	14 sub-cut	5 sub-cut
1 3/8" x 9 3/4"	41	28	24	8
1 3/8" x 10 5/8"	41	28	24	8
St. Louis Star block				
3 1/2" strip	4 sub-cut	3 sub-cut	3 sub-cut	1 sub-cut
	40 C	28 C	24 C	8 C
Border #3 strips	13 - 6 1/2"	11 – 6 1/2"	9 – 5"	6 – 4 1/2"
Binding strips	12 – 2 1/4"	10 – 2 1/4"	9 – 2 1/4"	6 – 2 1/4"
Dark #2				
Log Cabin block				
1 3/4" strips	21 sub-cut	14 sub-cut	12 sub-cut	4 sub-cut
1 3/4" x 8 1/2"	41	28	24	8
1 3/4"x 9 3/4"	41	28	24	8
St. Louis Star block				
3 1/2" strips	4 sub-cut	3 sub-cut	3 sub-cut	1 sub-cut
	40 C	28 C	24 C	8 C

Block Construction

Read all instructions before piecing.

St. Louis Star Blocks 1 and 2

Following the general piecing instructions beginning on page 21, make the number of St. Louis Star blocks 1 and 2 you need, referring to quilt information above.

Block 1 consists of: Two light C, four light D, two dark #2 C, four med. dark #2 A and four each B/Br, and four med. #1 A and four each B/Br.

Block 1

Block 2 consists of two light C, four light D, two dark #1 C, four med. dark #1 A and four each B/Br, and four med. #2 A and four each B/Br.

Log Cabin Block

The finished block should equal 10 1/2" and can be trimmed to that size when finished. Try to trim each log in the same place for consistency. I like to piece the logs in a chain fashion, sewing on the same sections at one time. Press to the last log sewn.

Block 2

 1. Sew med. light #2 - 1 3/4" x 2 1/8" to the bottom of light 2 1/8" square.

2. Sew med light #2 – 1 3/4" x 3 3/8" to the left side.

3. Sew med. light #1 – 1 3/8" x 3 3/8" to top.

4. Sew med. light #1 – 1 3/8" x 4 1/4" to right side.

5. Sew med. #2 -
1 3/4" x 4 1/4" to bottom.

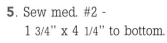

6. Sew med. #2 –
1 3/4" x 5 1/2" to
left side.

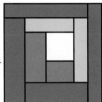

7. Sew med. #1 –
1 3/8" x 5 1/2" to top.

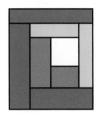

8. Sew med. #1 –
1 3/8" x 6 3/8"
to right side.

9. Sew med. dark #2 –
1 3/4" x 6 3/8"
to bottom.

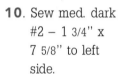

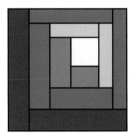

10. Sew med. dark
#2 – 1 3/4" x
7 5/8" to left
side.

11. Sew med. dark #1 -
1 3/8" x 7 5/8" to top.

12. Sew med. dark #1 – 1 3/8" x 8 1/2"
right side.

13. Sew dark #2 – 1 3/4" x 8 1/2"
to bottom.

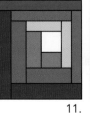   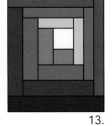

11.   12.

13.

14. Sew dark #2 - 1 3/4" x 9 3/4" to left
side.

15. Sew dark #1 - 1 3/8" x 9 3/4" to top.

16. Sew dark #1 – 1 3/8" x 10 5/8" to
right side.

Quilt Construction

Lay out blocks based on your quilt size,
alternating the log blocks and Blocks A
and B as in quilt layout illustration. The log
blocks alternate in direction with color #1 or
color #2 facing each other and the St. Louis
Star blocks all facing the same direction with
the dark corner squares running diagonally
across the quilt. See general quilt assembly
beginning on page 74 for sewing the
blocks and rows together.

Border Construction

Sew the light border strips together with
diagonal seams. Trim to quilt size and sew
on to the quilt.

Repeat with the medium dark #2 strips and
dark #1 strips for the second and third borders.

Follow finishing techniques on page 74 for
layering, basting, quilting, and binding.

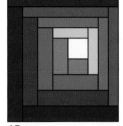

14.

15.

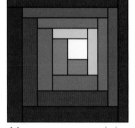

16.

St. Louis Courthouse Steps
Made and quilted by
Toby Lischko, 2008,
Wall size, 65 1/2'' x 65 1/2''
Fabrics courtesy of P&B Textiles,
Vintage Rose collection by Nancy Odom

This quilt combines the St. Louis Star block with a Courthouse Steps block. It's hard to tell where one block begins and the other ends. I quilted something different in each of the St. Louis Stars and a swirl design in the Courthouse Steps block.

St. Louis Courthouse Steps

I designed this wall quilt as my first commissioned quilt for P & B Textiles. I originally used a 7" block but decided that it should be a larger block to accommodate my templates. (See original quilt on page 82.) I chose a colorful medium print theme fabric that I could fussy-cut A of the St. Louis Star blocks. You do not have to fussy-cut A. Choose a dark and light for the Courthouse Steps block and background of the St. Louis Star block, and two contrasting fabrics for the star points.

QUILT INFORMATION

Quilt size: 62" x 62"

Block size: 10"

Number of blocks: 25 total
  13 St. Louis Stars
    4 light, 9 dark
  12 Courthouse Steps

Block layout: 5 x 5

Template size 10" on page 90

FABRIC REQUIREMENTS

Theme print -

Border #4 and St. Louis Star block	1 3/4 yards (If fussy cutting add 1 yard)
Light - Both blocks and border #2	1 3/8 yards
Dark - Both blocks, border #1, #3 and binding	2 1/2 yards
Fabric #1 (burgundy) - St. Louis Star block	1/2 yard
Fabric #2 (rose) - St. Louis Star block	1/2 yard
Back	4 yards
Batting	72" x 72"

Cutting Instructions

All strips are cut width of fabric (WOF).

Cut B/Br with contrast fabrics #1 and #2 placed wrong sides together with fabric #1 on top. Cut bigger strips first for the Courthouse Steps block and save the remainders to cut the smaller pieces.

FABRIC	NUMBER OF STRIPS	SUB-CUT
Theme print		
St. Louis Star block if fussy-cutting A	Cut 8 repeats of 13 different designs.	
	OR Cut (7) 2 5/8" strips	104 A
Border #4	Cut (6) 5"	
Border #3 corners	Cut (4) 1 1/2" x 1 1/2" (corners border 3)	
Light		
Light		
St. Louis Star block	Cut (2) 3 1/2" strips	16 C
	Cut (3) 2 3/4" strips	16 D
Courthouse Steps block	Cut (11) 1 3/4" strips	(24) 1 3/4" x 8" (24) 1 3/4" x 5 1/2" (24) 1 3/4" x 3"
Border #2	Cut (6) 1 1/2" strips	(4) 1 1/2" x 1 1/2" (corners border 1)
Dark		
St. Louis Star block	Cut (4) 3 1/2" strips Cut (3) 2 3/4" strips	36 C 36 D
Courthouse Steps block	Cut (16) 1 3/4" strips	(24) 1 3/4" x 10 1/2" (24) 1 3/4" x 8" (24) 1 3/4" x 5 1/2"
	Cut (1) 3"	(12) 3" x 3"
Border #1	Cut (6) 1 3/4" strips	
Border #3	Cut (6) 1 1/2" strips	(4) 1 1/2" x 1 1/2" (corners border 2)
Binding	Cut (7) 2 1/4" strips	
Contrast fabric #1		
St. Louis Star block	Cut (4) 3 1/2" strips	(104) B
Contrast fabric #2		
St. Louis Star block	Cut (4) 3 1/2" strips	(104) Br

Block Construction

Read all instructions before piecing.

St. Louis Star Block

Following the general piecing instructions, beginning on page 21, make nine blocks with the dark C and D (Block 1) and four blocks with the light C and D (Block 2).

Block 1

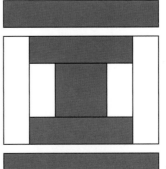

Block 2

Courthouse Steps block
Make 12

I like to piece the blocks chain style, sewing the same sections one right after the other. Clip apart and then sew on the next section. Press to section just sewn.

1. Sew two light 1 3/4" x 3" rectangles to the opposite sides of a 3" dark square. Make 12.

Step 1

2. Sew two dark 1 3/4" x 5 1/2" rectangles to the top and bottom.

Step 2

3. Sew two light 1 3/4" x 5 1/2" rectangles to opposite sides.

Step 3

4. Sew two dark 1 3/4" x 8" rectangles to top and bottom.

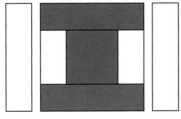

Step 4

Courthouse Steps block cont.

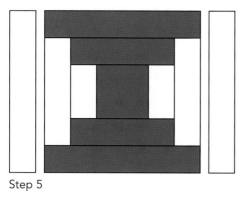

Step 5

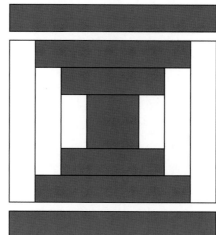

Step 6

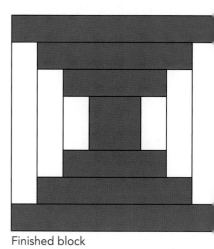

Finished block

5. Sew two light
   1 3/4" x 8" rectangles
   to opposite sides.

6. Sew two dark 1 3/4" x
   10 1/2" rectangles to
   top and bottom. Block
   should equal 10 1/2".

Quilt Construction

Lay out blocks, alternating the St. Louis Courthouse Steps blocks and St. Louis Star blocks, rotating the Courthouse Steps blocks to create the quilt layout.

See general quilt assembly on page 74 for sewing the blocks and rows together.

Border Construction

Follow general border instructions on page 77.

1. Sew the dark border strips together with diagonal seams. Trim to quilt length and width. Sew on sides. Sew the light 1 3/4" squares to each end of the remaining two strips and sew to top and bottom.

2. Repeat with the light 1 1/2" strips and dark 1 1/2" squares for the corners.

3. Repeat with the dark 1 1/2" strips and theme 1 1/2" squares for the corners.

4. Repeat with the theme 5" strips for the final border.

Follow finishing techniques on page 74 for layering, basting, quilting, and binding.

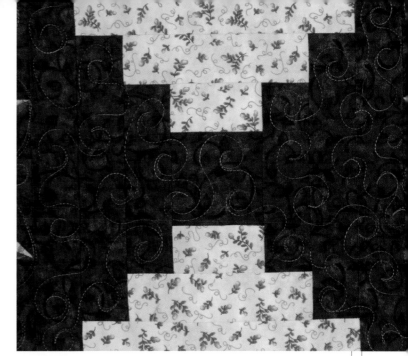

Border detail

Courthouse Steps

Assembly
Diagram

Midnight In The Butterfly Garden

I found this large butterfly border stripe in a quilt shop during one of my teaching engagements. I did not want to cut it up because it was so beautiful. I wondered what it would look like in a horizontal bar quilt with the bar as the whole stripe and the alternating bar a St. Louis Star block on-point. I found coordinating prints (dark, medium for setting triangles, and two contrasting prints for the St. Louis Star) and another small stripe for the border. I fussy-cut the center of the block from the small border stripe (though you do not need to). If you choose a small border stripe, make sure that you have four stripes to cut for the length of the borders after fussy-cutting on the other border stripes. By fussy-cutting in the exact same place for each block, the quilt seems to have some continuity. You can use a panel or large print for the plain bars. You should be able to get four bars from the length of the fabric. If not, you will need to add an extra length to your fabric requirements. This is a good quilt for large prints.

QUILT INFORMATION

Quilts size: 57" x 80"

Block size: 8 1/2"

Number of blocks: 12

Block layout: Horizontal bar

Template size: 8 1/2" A – D, on page 94.

FABRIC REQUIREMENTS

Theme print -

Large print or stripe (at least 8 1/2" wide) for bars	1 5/8 yards
Small border stripe for center of St. Louis Star block and border	2 5/8 yards
Dark – Sashing between bars, block background and border #1	1 1/2 yards
Contrast fabric #1 (purple), St. Louis Star block	3/8 yard
Contrast fabric #2 (green), St. Louis Star block	3/8 yard
Medium print for setting triangles	1 1/8 yards
Back	5 yards
Batting	64" x 87"

Midnight in the Butterfly Garden
Made and quilted by Toby Lischko, 2008
Lap size, 57" x 80"

I wanted to show off the large butterfly panel by featuring it in the alternating bars of this horizontal bar quilt. I fussy-cut the center of the St. Louis Star block using the border stripe at the same place in each star. I quilted around the butterflies and did swirls and feathers in the St. Louis Star.

Cutting Instructions

All strips are cut width of fabric (WOF).

Cut B/Br with contrast fabrics #1 and #2 placed wrong sides together with fabric #1 on top. Cut the large print for the horizontal bar lengthwise along the selvage edge for one long piece.

* *Note:* Before cutting the large print for the bars, piece the St. Louis Star bars and measure. It should measure 48 1/2". If not, cut to your own personal measurement. Do the same with the 1" dark strips.

**QTS refers to quarter-square triangles, squares cut two times diagonally. HST refers to half-square triangles, squares cut one time diagonally.

FABRIC	NUMBER OF STRIPS	SUB-CUT
Border print		
St. Louis Star block		
If fussy-cutting A	Cut 8 repeats of 12 designs.	
Template A	OR Cut (5) 2 3/8" strips	96 A
Border #2	Cut (2) 4 1/2" x 94"	
	Cut (2) 4 1/2" x 64"	
	Or the width of your stripe	
*Large print or stripe	(4) 48 1/2" x 8 1/2"	
Dark		
St. Louis Star block		
3" strips	4	48 C
2 3/8" strips	3	48 D
1" strips for Border #1	8	
1" strips for sashing	8	
2 1/4" strips for binding	8	
Contrast fabric #1		
St. Louis Star block		
3" strips	3	96 B
Contrast fabric #2		
St. Louis Star block		
3" strips	3	96 Br
Medium print for	Cut (5) 13 1/4" squares	18 QST**
setting triangles	Cut (6) 6 7/8" squares	12 HST**

Block Construction

Read all instructions before piecing.

St. Louis Star Block

Following the basic star construction beginning on page 18, make twelve blocks.

Quilt Construction

Lay out blocks, quarter-square triangles (QST) and half-square triangles (HST) according to the quilt layout illustration. Piece in diagonal rows described on page 75. Make three sets.

Trim the large 8 1/2'' bars to 48 1/2''. (*See note on p. 50.)

Sew the nine 1'' dark strips together with diagonal seams. Trim to six 48 1/2'' lengths (* See note on p. 77.)

See general quilt assembly on p. 74 for sewing the block bars, sashing, and solid bars together. Press to sashing.

Border Construction

1. Sew the seven dark 1'' border strips together with diagonal seams. Trim to two quilt lengths and two widths plus 14''.

2. Sew the seven 4 1/2'' border strips together with diagonal seams. Trim to two quilt lengths and two widths plus 14''.

3. Match centers of the dark 1'' strips and 4 1/2'' strips, pin and sew together. Press to the larger border.

4. Match the centers of the dark and striped border strip sets to quilt top, then pin and sew following the general border instructions for mitered corners on page 77.

Follow techniques beginning on page 80 for layering, basting, quilting, and binding.

Mitered borders

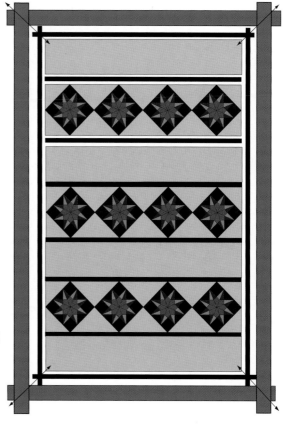

Ornamental Stars
Made and quilted by
Toby Lischko, 2005
Large wall size, 72" x 72"
Fabrics courtesy of Timeless Treasures,
Katerina collection.

I designed this quilt for *Quilt it for Christmas*, 2005, Primedia Publication (now known as CKMedia). It shows off the versatility of the St. Louis Star block in three different fabric placements.

Ornamental Stars

This is a wonderful holiday quilt. I chose black, cream, red, green, red and black prints and a border print to pull it all together. You can start with a border print or multi-color theme print for the border and then choose a light, dark, two contrasting colors and a second dark. There are three versions of the St. Louis Star block surrounded by a double sash with a four-patch as a cornerstone. It's all about fabric placement on the block.

QUILT INFORMATION

Quilt size: 72" x 72"	
Block size: 12"	
Number of blocks: 13	
Block layout: On-point 3 x 3	
Template size: 12" on page 91.	

FABRIC REQUIREMENTS

Theme (stripe)	2 1/2 yards
Print	or 1 5/8 yards
Light	2 3/8 yards
Contrast #1 (red)	1 3/8 yards
Contrast #2 (green)	7/8 yards
Dark #1 (black)	2 yards
Dark #2 (black/red)	3/4 yards
Backing	4 1/2 yards
Batting	75" x 75"

Cutting Instructions

All strips are cut width of fabric (WOF).

*IMPORTANT: For B and Br, cut the strip in half (2 pieces 20" – 22" long) and place both right sides up for B and both wrong sides up for Br. You will be cutting all B at one time, then all Br at the same time. QST refers to quarter square triangle (setting triangles), a square cut twice diagonally. HST refers to half square triangle (corner triangle), a square cut once diagonally.

FABRIC	NUMBER OF STRIPS	SUB-CUT
Theme fabric		
Border strips	(4) 85" lengths or	
	10 – 5 1/2" strips	
Light		
4 1/8" strips	4	20 B*
		20 Br*
		16 C
		16A
3 1/8" strips	2	16 D
	(2) 21" squares	8 QST
	(2) 12 1/4" squares	4 HST
Contrast #1		
4 1/8" strips	3	48 B*
3 1/8" strips	2	16 Br*
1 1/2" strips for sashing and cornerstones	14	20 A
Contrast #2		
3 1/8" strips	3	36 A
4 1/8" strips	3	16 D
Cornerstones		
1 1/2" strips for cornerstone	2	16 C
Dark #1		
3 1/8" strips	3	32A
4 1/8" strips	4	36 B*
1 1/2" strips for sashing	12	68 Br*
2 1/4" strips for binding	8	
Dark #2		
3 1/8" strips	2	20 D
4 1/8" strips	3	20 C

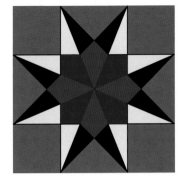

Block 1

Block 2

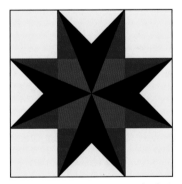

Block 3

Block Construction
Read all instructions before piecing.

St. Louis Star blocks 1, 2, and 3
Construct five of block 1, four of block 2, and four of block 3 using the illustrations above and following the general piecing instructions on page 18.

BLOCK 1 consists of four contrast #1 A, four contrast #2 A, four light B, four light Br, four dark #1 B, four dark #1 Br, four dark #2 C, and four dark #2 D.

BLOCK 2 consists of four light A, four dark #1 A, eight contrast #1 B, eight dark #1 Br, four contrast #2 C, and four contrast #2 D.

BLOCK 3 consists of four contrast #2 A, four dark #1 A, four contrast #1 B, four contrast #1 Br, four dark #1 B, four dark #1 Br, four light C, and four light D.

Sash Construction

1. Sew twelve 1 1/2'' dark #1 strips to twelve 1 1/2'' contrast #1 strips. Press to dark. Sub-cut the strip sets into 36 – 12 1/2'' sections.

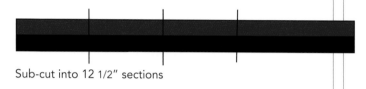

Sub-cut into 12 1/2'' sections

2. Sew two 1 1/2'' contrast #1 strips to two 1 1/2'' contrast #2 strips. Press to contrast #2. Cut into 48 – 1 1/2'' sections.

Sub-cut into 1 1/2'' sections

3. Sew two 1 1/2'' sections together to create a four patch. Make 24 four-patches.

Make a four-patch with two 1 1/2'' sections

Quilt Construction

Lay out blocks 1, 2, 3, the light setting triangles (QST), light corner triangles (HST), 12 1/2'' sashing strips and four-patches following the quilt layout.
Rotate the sashing and cornerstone four-patches as in the illustration. Use the photo on page 52 to help with block and sashing directions. Sew together following one of the on-point setting instructions on page 76.

Miter corners   Ornamental Stars quilt layout

Border Construction

Sew the ten 5 1/2'' border strips together. If you are using a stripe, sew a straight seam. If it is a print, use a diagonal seam. Trim to four 85'' borders. Sew borders on the quilt following miter instructions on page 77.

Follow the techniques beginning on page 80 for layering, basting, quilting, and binding.

Autumn in New England

I made this quilt with a wonderful fabric collection called "Autumn in New England" by P&B Textiles. I started with a theme fabric and picked six coordinating fabrics from very dark to very light. Find a theme fabric that you like that has lots of colors and pick a light, a dark, and four colors that coordinate with it. They should be small prints or tone-on-tones. The St. Louis Star block in this quilt has two triangles in the corners instead of a square. It creates a Snowball block effect that make the blocks flow across the quilt in a bowtie effect.

QUILT INFORMATION

Quilt size	King	Double/Queen	Twin	Lap
Finished size	108" x 108"	89" x 101"	74" x 94"	61" x 73"
Number of blocks	49 total	42 total	30 total	20 total
Block size: 12"	24 St. Louis Star	21 St. Louis Star	15 St. Louis Star	10 St. Louis Star
	25 Double four-patch	21 Double four-patch	15 Double four-patch	10 Double four-patch
Block layout	7 x 7	6 x 7	5 x 6	4 x 5
Template size: 12" on page 91.				

FABRIC REQUIREMENTS (YARDS)

	King	Double/Queen	Twin	Lap
Theme print – Border #3	2 3/4 yards	2 1/2 yards	2 1/8 yards	1 3/4 yards
Light - Both blocks	2 1/8 yards	1 3/4 yards	1 3/8 yards	1 yard
Dark - Both blocks, border #2 and binding	2 3/4 yards	2 1/2 yards	2 yards	1 5/8 yards
Fabric #1 (gold) - Both blocks	1 1/4 yards	1 1/8 yards	1 yards	5/8 yards
Fabric #2 (red) - St. Louis Star block, border #1 and border cornerstones	3 1/8 yards	2 1/4 yards	1 7/8 yards	1 3/8 yards
Fabric #3 (teal) - Both blocks	2 1/4 yards	2 yards	1 3/8 yards	1 yard
Fabric #4 (green) - St. Louis Star block	1 1/4 yards	1 1/8 yards	7/8 yard	5/8 yard
Back	9 2/3 yards	8 1/8 yards	5 2/3 yards	3 7/8 yards
Batting	King	Queen	Twin	Twin

Autumn in New England
Made and quilted by Toby Lischko, 2008
Lap size, 61" x 73"
Fabrics courtesy of P&B Textiles,
Autumn in New England collection.

I used this fabric collection in a commissioned quilt for P&B with the same name. I loved all of the colors in the border print and wanted to use them all in the quilt. They are the same small print in five different colorways. By adding half-square triangles to the corners of the St. Louis Star block you can create a large bowtie effect. Since this was a very busy design, I quilted an all-over pattern on it.

Cutting Instructions

All strips are cut width of fabric (WOF).

Cut B/Br with fabrics #3 or #4 placed wrong sides together (not #3 and #4). In other words, the same fabrics will be placed wrong sides together so you will get B and Br at the same time from the same fabrics.

*Indicates that Template D is cut with the short edge on straight-of-grain for this quilt.

FABRIC	KING	QUEEN	TWIN	LAP
Strip size, and sub-cut size	Number of strips and sub-cuts	Number of strips and sub-cuts	Number of strips and sub-cuts	Number of strips and sub-cuts
Light				
Double four-patch				
3 1/2" strips	11 sub-cut	8 sub-cut	6 sub-cut	4 sub-cut
3 1/2" x 3 1/2"	100	84	60	40
2" strips	10 sub-cut	9 sub-cut	6 sub-cut	4 sub-cut
2" x 2"	200	168	120	80
St. Louis Star				
4 1/8" strips	3 sub-cut	3 sub-cut	2 sub-cut	2 sub-cut
	48 D*	42 D*	30 D*	20 D*
Dark (black)				
Double four-patch				
3 1/2"	5 sub-cut	4 sub-cut	3 sub-cut	2 sub-cut
3 1/2" x 3 1/2"	50	42	30	20
St. Louis Star				
4 1/8" strips	3 sub-cut	3 sub-cut	2 sub-cut	2 sub-cut
	48 D*	42 D*	30 D*	20 D*
3 1/8" strip	7 sub-cut	6 sub-cut	5 sub-cut	3 sub-cut
	96 A	84 A	60 A	40 A
Border #2	(9) 2 3/8" strips	(8) 1 3/4" strips	(7) 1 5/8" strips	(6) 1 1/2" strips
Binding				
2 1/4" strips	11	10	9	7
Fabric #1 (gold)				
Double four-patch				
3 1/2" strips	5 sub-cut	4 sub-cut	3 sub-cut	2 sub-cut
3 1/2" x 3 1/2"	50	42	30	20
St. Louis Star				
3 1/8"	7 sub-cut	6 sub-cut	5 sub-cut	3 sub-cut
	96 A	84 A	60 A	40 A

FABRIC	KING	QUEEN	TWIN	LAP
Fabric. #2 (red)				
St. Louis Star block				
4 1/8" strips	6 sub-cut	6 sub-cut	5 sub-cut	3 sub-cut
	96 D*	84 D*	60 D*	40 D*
3 1/8" strips	8 sub-cut	7 sub-cut	4 sub-cut	3 sub-cut
	96 D	84 D	60 D	40 D
Border #1	(9) 3 1/4" strips	(8) 2 1/2" strips	(7) 2 1/4" strips	(6) 2" strips
Border corners (4)	12 1/2" squares	9" squares	8" squares	7" squares
Fabric. #3 (teal)				
Double four-patch				
3 1/2" strips	10 sub-cut	8 sub-cut	6 sub-cut	4 sub-cut
3 1/2" x 3 1/2"	100	84	60	40
2" strips	5 sub-cut	5 sub-cut	3 sub-cut	2 sub-cut
2" x 2"	100	84	60	40
St. Louis Star block				
4 1/8" strips	7 sub-cut	6 sub-cut	4 sub-cut	3 sub-cut
	96 B/96 B	84 B/84 Br	60 B/60Br	40 B/40 Br
Fabric #4 (green)				
Double four-patch				
2" strips	5 sub-cut	5 sub-cut	3 sub-cut	2 sub-cut
2" x 2"	100	84	60	40
St. Louis Star block				
4 1/8" strips	7 sub-cut	6 sub-cut	4 sub-cut	3 sub-cut
	96 B/96 Br	84 B/84 Br	60 B/60 Br	40 B/40 Br
Stripe or theme				
Border #3	(9) 7 7/8"strips	(8) 5 3/4" strips	(7) 5 1/8" strips	(6) 4 1/2" strips

Block Construction

Read all instructions before piecing.

St. Louis Star block

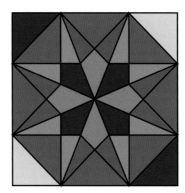

Sew the following pairs of D* triangles to create the corners of the block (HSTs – half-square triangles) and use in place of C in the basic star construction: Dark/fabric #2 and light/fabric #2. Make the following number of HST based on the size of the quilt, starting with the lap size (20/30/42/48) for each color combination.

Construct the number of blocks for your quilt size with each the colors below, following the general piecing instructions and photo of the block.

Each block consists of:
Four dark A, four #1 A, four #3 B, four #3 Br, four #4 B, four #4 Br, two HST Dark/fabric #2 (in place of C), two HST Light/fabric #2 (in place of C) and four #2 D.

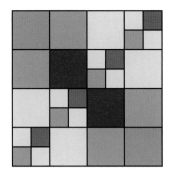

Double Four-patch Block

I like to piece the small and large four-patches in a "string," also called chain stitching, (one right after the other). Directions are given for the lap quilt. Numbers of each section for the twin, double/queen, and king size quilts are in the parentheses in order.

UNIT 1

1. Layout one fabric #1, two fabric #3, and one dark 3 1/2" squares as illustrated. Fold the right column of fabrics right sides together to the left column fabrics.

Tip: Stack the same fabrics on top of each other and sew one right after the other. Clip every other thread so that the four-patches are attached. Press to dark and fabric #1. Match centers and sew seam. Split center seam threads and press all seams clockwise. Make 20 (30/42/50).

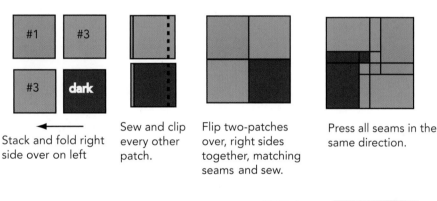

Stack and fold right side over on left

Sew and clip every other patch.

Flip two-patches over, right sides together, matching seams and sew.

Press all seams in the same direction.

UNIT 2

2. Layout one fabric #3, one fabric #4, and two light 2" squares as illustrated. Repeat directions from step 1. Press to fabric #3 and #4 and then counter-clockwise. Make 40 (60/84/100).

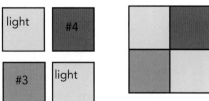

UNIT 3

3. Layout two light 3 1/2" squares and two Unit 2, making sure that fabric #4 square is in the upper right corner as illustrated. Sew as in step 1. Press to light 3 1/2" squares, then counter-clockwise.

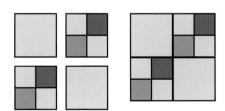

4. Lay out two Unit 1 and two Unit 3 as illustrated. Sew as in step 1. Press to Unit 1, then counter-clockwise.

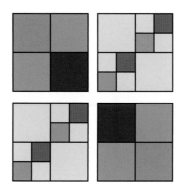 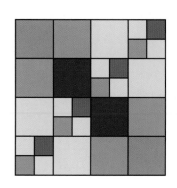

Quilt Construction

Lay out blocks based on your quilt size, alternating the Double Four-Patch blocks and St. Louis Star blocks. All blocks face in the same direction. See general quilt assembly beginning on pages 74 for sewing the blocks and rows together.

Border Construction

1. Sew the dark border strips together with diagonal seams. Trim to quilt length and width.

2. Repeat with the fabric #2 and theme print. Sew border strips together starting with dark and ending with the theme print. Press towards outer borders.

3. Sew side strips to left and right sides of quilt. Sew the 7" (8", 9", 12 1/2") fabric #2 squares to each end of the remaining two border sections and sew to top and bottom matching centers and seams.

Follow finishing techniques beginning on page 74 for layering, basting, quilting, and binding.

Psychedelic Stars
Made and quilted by
Toby Lischko, 2008
Small wall size, 25 1/2" x 25 1/2"

I like collecting wild prints and I wondered what the border fabric would look like cut up in the center of the St. Louis Star block since it was so busy. I was pleasantly surprised at the outcome. I tried to focus on the bright colors within the design so that they would be more noticeable. I quilted in-the-ditch.

Psychedelic Stars

Sometimes you purchase fabrics and you are not sure what to do with them. I have had the fabric in this border and block for some time and wasn't sure how I would use it in a quilt. The overall design on the fabric was so busy, I wasn't sure if it would even make a difference to the center of the stars. After fussy-cutting piece A and putting the pieces on my design wall, they still did not show up very clearly. By using a color in the star points that is in the feature fabric, you can accentuate specific colors in it. It makes those colors stand out. I have seen this block made with so-called "ugly" fabrics, those fabrics that you look back on and say "Why did I buy that?" Start with the feature fabric and pick different accent colors for each block, one background fabric to pull it together, and one of the accents for the sashing.

QUILT INFORMATION

Quilt size: 25 1/2" x 25 1/2", small wall size

Block size: 10"

Number of blocks: 4

Block layout: Straight set with sashing.

Template size: 10" on page 90.

FABRIC REQUIREMENTS

Small theme print for border and Template A	1 yard if fussy-cutting 1/2 yard if not fussy-cutting
Three accent colors	Fat quarter
Light background	1/2 yard
Dark accent for star, sashing, and binding	1/2 yard
Backing	7/8 yard or 28" x 28"
Batting	28" x 28"

Cutting Instructions

All strips are cut width of fabric (WOF).

Cut B/Br with the same color fabric placed wrong sides together.

FABRIC	NUMBER OF STRIPS	SUB-CUT
Theme print	(2) 2 5/8" strip or fussy-cut	32 A
Border	(4) 2 1/2"	
Fat quarters (FQ)		
St. Louis Star blocks	(1) 3 1/2" strip from each	
	FQ	8 B and 8 Br from each FQ
Sashing cornerstones		(4) 1" x 1" from 1 FQ
		(5) 1" x 1" from 1 FQ
Dark		
St. Louis Star block	(1) 3 1/2" strip	8 B and 8 Br
Sashing	(4) 1" strips	(12) 1" x 10 1/2"
Binding	(3) 2 1/2" strips	
Background		
St. Louis Star blocks	(2) 3 1/2"	16 C
	(2) 2 3/4"	16 D

Block Construction

Read all instructions before piecing

St. Louis Star Blocks

Construct four blocks with each of the colors using B/BR, theme fabric A, and background C and D following the general piecing instructions.

Quilt Construction

Following quilt layout, sew the stars, sashing, and cornerstones together. Press to sashing strips.

Border Construction

Cut 2 1/2" border strips to quilt size and sew on, following general directions beginning on page 77.

Follow the finishing techniques beginning on page 74 for layering, basting, quilting, and binding.

Falling Stars

I love finding fabrics that have different colorways. This is a Thimbleberries fabric collection from RJR that has three different colors of the same leaves. I was able to find the same area on each colorway and fussy-cut the centers. I then surrounded the stars with the same dark, medium, and light prints and set the blocks on point in vertical bars with half-square and quarter-square triangles of the same prints I used in the center blocks. I chose the darkest print for the final border. If you can not find three fabrics with the same print, look for similar medium—size prints in different colors and add coordinating colors in small prints or tone-on-tones.

QUILT INFORMATION

Quilt size: 64" x 81"	
Block size: 12"	
Number of blocks: 11 full and 2 half blocks	
Block layout: On-point vertical bar	
Template size: 12" on page 91	

FABRIC REQUIREMENTS

Color #1- blocks, setting triangles and border #3	2 1/2 yards
Color #2 – blocks and setting triangles	1 1/4 yards
Color #3 – blocks and setting triangles	1 1/4 yards
Light – blocks and border #2	1 1/2 yards
Medium - blocks	7/8 yards
Dark – blocks, border #1 and binding	1 1/8 yards
Backing	5 yards
Batting	74" x 91"

Cutting Instructions

All strips are cut width of fabric (WOF).

Cut B/Br with dark and medium fabrics placed wrong sides together and medium fabric on top.

Falling Stars
Made and quilted by Toby Lischko, 2008
Lap size, 64" x 81"
Fabrics courtesy of RJR Fabrics,
Thimbleberries collection.

This quilt features three different colorways of the same print. Made as a vertical bar quilt, it goes together quickly. I fussy-cut the center of the St. Louis Star blocks using all three coordinating prints in the same place on each fabric. I sometimes get my ideas on how to quilt it by looking at the fabrics. In the zigzags and the border I outlined the leaves and the St. Louis Stars have feathery leaves in the points.

FABRIC	NUMBER OF STRIPS	SUB-CUT
From each of color #1, #2, and #3	32A from each of 2 prints and 34A from each of 1 print	
Fussy-cut		
OR 3 1/8" strips	3 each	32A from 2 prints and 34A from 1 print (center 3 stars and 2 half stars
Color #1		
Setting triangles	(2) 18 1/4" squares	6 QST
Corner triangles	(2) 9 3/8" squares	4 HST
Border #3	(8) 5 1/2" strips	
Color #2 and #3		
Setting triangles	(2) 18 1/4" squares	7 QST
Corner triangles	(1) 9 3/8" squares	2 HST
Dark		
4 1/8" strips	4	96 Br
2 1/4" strips for binding	8	
Medium		
4 1/8" strips	4	96 B
1 1/2" strips for border #1	6	
Light		
3 1/8" strips	4	52 D
4 1/8" strips	6	46 C
1 1/2" strips for border #2	7	

Block Construction

Read all instructions before piecing.

St. Louis Star blocks 1, 2, and 3

Construct four blocks with colors #2 and #3 in A and three blocks with color #1 in A following the general piecing instructions on page 21.

Block 1   Block 2   Block 3

Two St. Louis Star blocks will be half blocks of color #1 in A. You will need 5A, 4B, 4Br, 1C, and 4D per half block.

St. Louis Star Half-block Construction

1. Following general piecing instructions, piece one Group 1 and two Group 2.

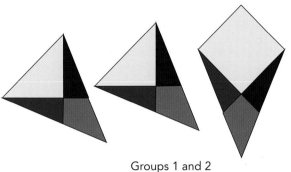

Groups 1 and 2

2. Sew these together with Group 1 in the center and press seams open.

Sew together

3. Sew A to B and A to Br as illustrated. Press A/B to A and A/Br to Br.

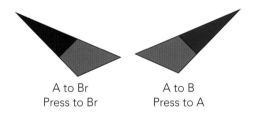

A to Br
Press to Br

A to B
Press to A

4. Sew A/Br on the left side of the group and A/B on the right. Press open.

Sew A/Br on left
A/B on right

5. Sew D to each side as illustrated, lining up the edges of the triangle to the edges of B and Br.

6. Trim block along the bottom edge of the triangles with a ruler and the rotary cutter.

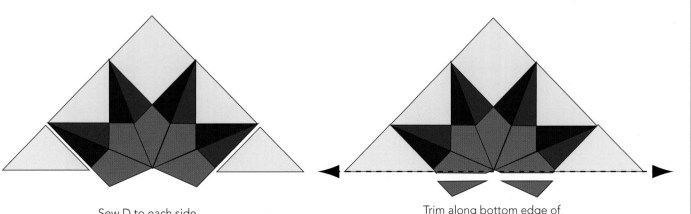

Sew D to each side

Trim along bottom edge of the triangles

Quilt Construction

Following quilt layout, sew the half-square triangles (HST) and quarter-square triangles (QST) in long horizontal rows, making sure to keep color #1, color #2, and color #3 on the proper sides of the row. I placed color #1 blocks in the center, color #2 and #3 on the left and right. Use on-point layout instructions on page 75 for sewing blocks together.

Border Construction

Following the border instructions on page 77, sew the 1 1/2'' dark strips together, trim two to the length of the quilt and sew on sides. Trim two strips from the remainder, to the width of the quilt and sew to top and bottom. Repeat for the 1 1/2'' light and 5 1/2'' color #1 strips. Follow finishing techniques beginning on page 74 for layering, basting, quilting and binding.

Finishing
Basic layout, border construction, and binding techniques

BASIC LAYOUTS

For variety, I have chosen many different quilt layouts in this book from straight sets, on-point sets, and horizontal bars to vertical bars. With the St. Louis Star block, it adapts to any type of setting. The different types of layouts are listed in each pattern instruction under the basic quilt information. There are straight set layouts with and without sashing.

STRAIGHT SET LAYOUTS

When sewing straight sets, sew rows across first, press all seams to the left every other row and to the right on the alternating rows. Then sew the rows together. Try to press to the side of the least resistance (the least pieced blocks). If there are two blocks where the stars meet, press the seams open for less bulk.

When sewing straight sets with sashing strips, treat the sashing strips and cornerstones (pieced or unpieced) as a row and press towards the sashing strips.

Straight Sets

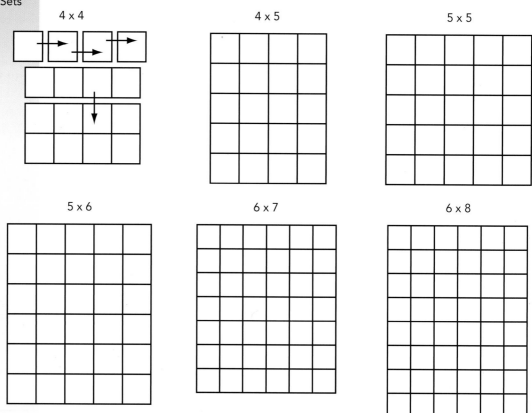

4 x 4

4 x 5

5 x 5

5 x 6

6 x 7

6 x 8

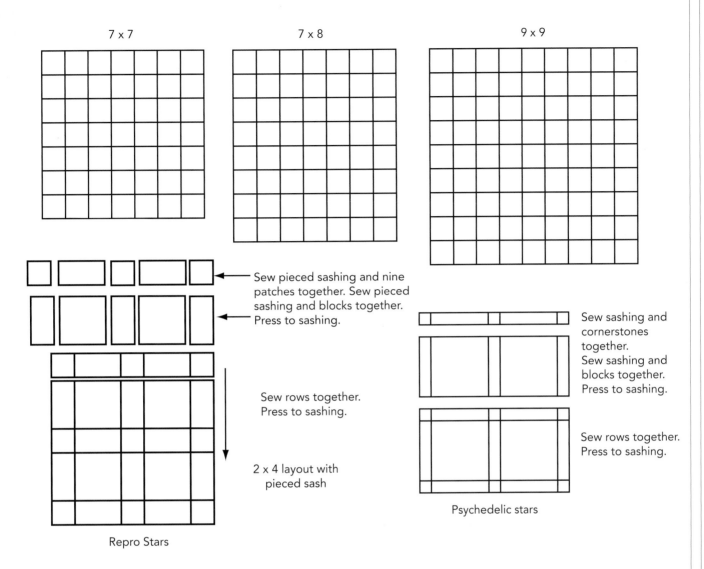

7 x 7   7 x 8   9 x 9

Sew pieced sashing and nine patches together. Sew pieced sashing and blocks together. Press to sashing.

Sew rows together. Press to sashing.

2 x 4 layout with pieced sash

Repro Stars

Sew sashing and cornerstones together.
Sew sashing and blocks together. Press to sashing.

Sew rows together. Press to sashing.

Psychedelic stars

ON-POINT LAYOUTS

There are three types of on-point layouts used in the book: on-point with sashing (*Ornamental Stars*, page 52), on-point horizontal bar (*Midnight in the Butterfly Garden*, page 48), and on-point vertical bar (*Falling Stars*, page 68). For on-point layouts in the bar quilts, sew each row as a unit, in diagonal sets, sewing blocks to setting triangles. Press seams in opposite directions from section to section.

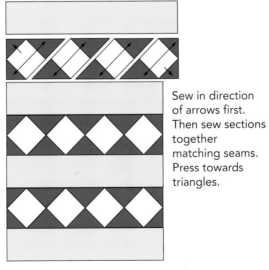

Sew in direction of arrows first. Then sew sections together matching seams. Press towards triangles.

Midnight in the Butterfly Garden

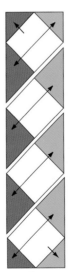
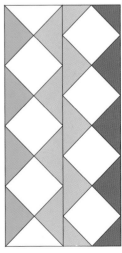

Falling Stars

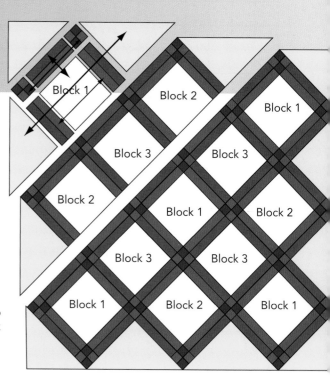

The *Ornamental Stars* quilt can be pieced in two different ways. Treat the sashing rows as the block rows as in the straight set piecing directions, pressing to the sashing. Sew the rows together in diagonal sets with the setting triangles and corner triangles.

Sew diagonal rows together. Sew the sashing to the four-patches. Then blocks to sashing, finishing with the setting triangles on each end of the block rows. Press to setting triangles. Press to sashing strips. Then sew block row to sashing row. Press to sashing rows. Sew corners on last.

Sew corner as in option 1 illustration. Make 4. Sew center nine blocks, sashing, and cornerstones together; sewing sashing rows first then sashing plus blocks. Sew rows together to create the center nine blocks. Follow same pressing instructions as in option 1.

Square quilts, that have on-point settings, can be pieced in an easier manner. Treat the center of the *Ornamental Stars* quilt as a nine-patch (three by three blocks) and sew the blocks together (with the sashing and cornerstones), pressing towards the sashing strips. Sew the corner units together (blocks, sashing, setting triangles and corners). Before pressing, check to see what direction the seams are going on the center unit, then press seams in the opposite direction on the corner unit and sew to center unit. Press seam to sash.

Stars Over St. Louis, page 30, is in a class by itself. It is a medallion style quilt, with a large center star on-point, surrounded by four half stars, which are simply triangle corners sewn to the center star.

Border Treatments

Sometimes thinking about what kind of border to put on a quilt is the hardest part of the design process. Do I do a pieced border, mitered border, or corner treatment? How many strips do I need in the border? How wide should I make it? Actually, I do not use any mysterious math formula to figure it out. I just do what is pleasing to my eye. If I have a border stripe, I will usually do a mitered corner, but there is no hard or fast rule. I always tell my students, "Do what makes you happy. There are no quilt police to tell you that you did something wrong on your own quilt." My favorite border treatment, one which I feel is the easiest to piece, is to make two or three strips, cut them all the length and width of the quilt, sew them together and put a pieced block or square in the corners. This way I only have to measure the quilt once through the center both horizontally and vertically. I used this method in the *Autumn in New England* quilt, p. 56. As the different quilt sizes got larger, I just increased the size of the border strips and the corners.

Basic Border Construction

I used to measure the borders, decide how many strips I needed to piece one side, sew those strips together, measure and cut, then repeat for the other sides. A few years ago, I started working with Ann Anderson, who used to own Quiltwoman.com, and she wrote some of my pattern directions for me. She suggested you piece all of the border strips at one time and then cut what you needed for each side from the long strip. I find this method much better, plus it usually uses less cut strips. Sew all the same width border strips together with a diagonal or bias seam. Use a smaller stitch when sewing and press these seams open.

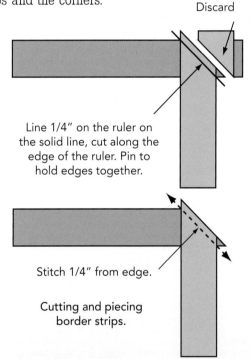

Discard

Line 1/4" on the ruler on the solid line, cut along the edge of the ruler. Pin to hold edges together.

Stitch 1/4" from edge.

Cutting and piecing border strips.

It is very important to measure the quilt before sewing the borders on. You don't want your longarm quilter angry or frustrated because the borders are too big for the quilt! Always measure the border through the center of the pieced quilt. If it is a large quilt, lay the quilt on the floor or a bed and place the border strips across the quilt. Then mark or clip the strips at the edges of the quilt.

Then take the border strips to your cutting table and use a rotary cutter and ruler to cut a straight edge at the clip.

Lay border strips across the center of the quilt and clip at edges of the quilt top on both sides and trim or measure through the center and cut border strips to this length.

Measuring border strips

When sewing on the borders it is important to match the centers and ends of the strips and the quilt and pin, pin, pin. To match the centers, fold the border with wrong sides together and the quilt right sides together to create a crease at the center of both. The two creases will fit into each other and make it easier to match and pin the center points. Pin each end and ease the remainder of the quilt or border, pinning frequently. If there is one side that seems to have a little more easing to it, place it on the bottom towards the sewing machine when sewing. The feed dogs on the machine will help ease the excess fabric. If the quilt is large, also match the quarter points. Repeat this process for as many borders that you have. Always press towards the last border sewn. (Well, that is not a hard fast rule, but one I usually follow.)

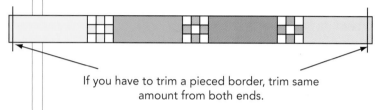

If you have to trim a pieced border, trim same amount from both ends.

Trimming pieced borders

For pieced borders, the accuracy of your blocks is important because you are sewing a border to a specific size. The *Reproduction Stars* quilt, page 24, has a pieced border. You should still measure through the center of the quilt and if you do have to make any adjustments to the border, make them at both ends, cutting equal amounts off each side.

For mitered borders it is important to cut enough extra fabric to allow for the mitered corner. Use the following rule of thumb: Take the border width measurement times two and add an extra 2", then add that to the quilt measurement. For example: Finished border size is 5" so 5 x 2 = 10 + 2 = 12. Therefore you will cut a border strip that is the width of the quilt plus 12".

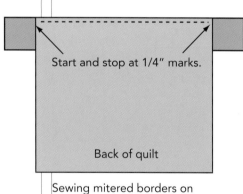

Start and stop at 1/4" marks.

Back of quilt

Sewing mitered borders on

When sewing on the mitered borders, you still need to mark the width of the quilt on the strips with pins. Fold the strip in half, place it on the halfway mark on the quilt (remember you still measure through the center of the quilt) and place a pin on each end (half the measurement of the quilt top). These pins will be used to match the quilt edges. Mark 1/4" in from the edge of the quilt on the back of the corners and then sew with the border strip on the bottom towards the sewing machine. This way you can see where to start and stop stitching and backstitch at the 1/4" mark. Sew on all four borders before mitering the corners. Press towards border.

For a perfect mitered corner, turn the quilt face up. Lay the border strip on the top of the quilt straight to the right. Take the right border strip, fold the end of the strip, starting at the 1/4" seam intersection, under to create a 45° angle. The two border strips will be right sides together and directly on top of one another. Take a square ruler with a 45° line and place in on the corner to check the "squareness" of it. The angle on the border miter should be at the 45° mark on the ruler and the corner should be square along the edge of the ruler. Make any adjustments at this time with the top border strip, pulling or pushing, until it is completely square. Then place a couple of pins at the fold

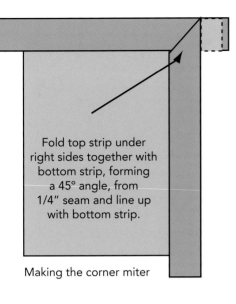

Fold top strip under right sides together with bottom strip, forming a 45° angle, from 1/4" seam and line up with bottom strip.

Making the corner miter

to hold the strips together and press it with an iron to make a sharp crease. Very carefully take out the pins and fold the quilt in half diagonally right sides together, being careful to keep the borders together (place a couple more pins to hold them right sides together). If you have trouble seeing the crease, use a marking utensil, to draw in the crease with a ruler. Pin the borders along the line and sew, backstitching from the 1/4" seam to the outside of the border strip along the marked line. Double check one last time to see if the corner is still square, using a square ruler, and make any adjustment if necessary. Trim seams to 1/4". Repeat with the other three borders. Press the seams open.

Pieced Backing

There are several options when piecing the backing. First, for large quilts, check with your longarm quilter, if you use one, to see if they prefer that the seams go horizontal or vertical to the quilt. They like the backs to be "squared off" (for example the top of the back is not larger than the bottom) so it is just as important to piece the back as even as the front. They will also tell you how much larger they like the back, usually from 4" to 8" larger than the front.

For the king–size quilts, you will need three widths of fabrics. Be sure to measure and cut each piece the same size and pin and sew them together with at least a 5/8" seam. If the selvages are larger, then use a bigger seam. Cut off the selvages and leave 1/4" seam after you sew. Press these seams open.

For some quilts you can use two widths plus a smaller width in the center and for others you will only need two pieces. You can save fabric by piecing the center piece.

Of course, don't discount using leftover scrap pieces on the back. Be sure when you piece them that the top and side edges are trimmed even.

Piecing backs

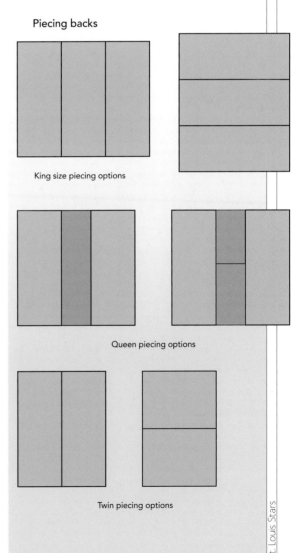

King size piecing options

Queen piecing options

Twin piecing options

Layering and Quilting

Layer the quilt top, batting, and backing. Baste using your favorite basting technique. If you have the quilt quilted by a longarm quilter, you do not need to baste the quilt. There are a variety of methods for basting. Before I got my longarm machine, I would spray baste the wall or smaller quilts. You can use safety pins, tacking gun, or iron on batting. If you have a large quilt, get your quilting friends together and have a basting party at your favorite quilt shop if you do not have a table big enough to work on. It makes the job go much faster and is definitely more fun!

There are many ways to quilt these quilts. Some you can quilt in-the-ditch (along the seam line). If you have a very busy print or design, such as in the Autumn in New England quilt, try an all-over design. Feathers make a nice touch in the log cabin blocks or flower designs in the corners of the star block. Be creative. I feel the design of the quilt (the blocks and kaleidoscope effect) is the most important part and the quilting should accent it or just hold it together. I don't like my quilting to overpower my designs because I want people to focus on the stars.

After quilting, trim the backing and batting even with the edge of the quilt. Square off the corners with a large square ruler.

Binding

Sew binding strips together with diagonal seams using the same technique as described on page 78 for piecing border strips. Fold binding strips lengthwise with wrong sides together and pin as you sew it to the quilt (no need to press). Match raw edges of binding to the front quilt edges starting about 1/3 down one side. It is a good idea to check placing the binding around the edge of the quilt to make sure that none of the seams end up on one of the corners. Using a 1/4" seam, start sewing 8" from the end of the strip and stop 1/4" before the corner. (Step 1)

Step 1

Matching raw edges of binding striips and quilt top, start stitching 8" down and backstitch at 1/4".

Fold strip up forming a 45° angle. (Step 2) Fold down matching the fold to the edge of the quilt. Sew from the edge and to the next 1/4" mark. (Step 3) Repeat the corner technique around the quilt.

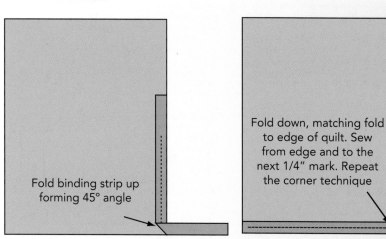

Fold binding strip up forming 45° angle

Step 2

Fold down, matching fold to edge of quilt. Sew from edge and to the next 1/4" mark. Repeat the corner technique

Step 3

Stop stitching 16" from the first stitching. Open the two strips (beginning and ending), fold the end of the strip to meet the beginning of the other strip and crease. Measure 2 1/4" from crease and trim off the remainder. The two end pieces will overlap by 2 1/4". Match edges, right sides together, at a 90° angle as you did when you sewed the strips together. Draw a diagonal line and stitch along the line. You will have to pull the strips out of the way of the quilt to do this. Trim to 1/4". Press the seam open. Pin and continue sewing the binding down.

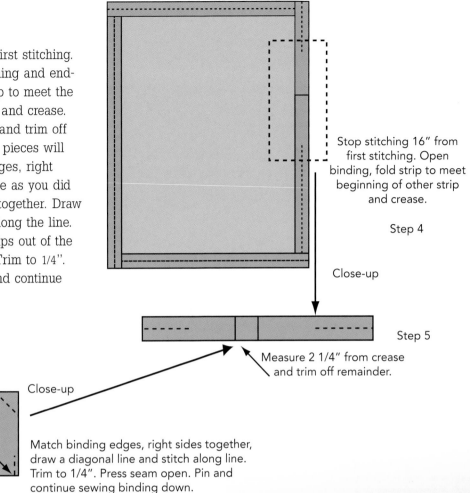

Stop stitching 16" from first stitching. Open binding, fold strip to meet beginning of other strip and crease.

Step 4

Close-up

Step 5

Measure 2 1/4" from crease and trim off remainder.

Close-up

Edges sewn

Step 6

Match binding edges, right sides together, draw a diagonal line and stitch along line. Trim to 1/4". Press seam open. Pin and continue sewing binding down.

Be sure to put a label on your quilt with your name, date and the name of anyone else who was involved with the making of it. You might also want to include if it was made for a special occasion and who it was made for.

Now for the most important part! Step back, take a look and admire your work. The finished quilt is always such an enjoyable experience for me. Usually it turns out much better than I expected. But most of all, the whole process for me is fun. Quilting should be fun, so enjoy your quilt and have fun making many more.

Gallery

St. Louis Courthouse Steps I
Made by Toby Lischko, 2002
Wall size, 46" x 46"
Fabrics courtesy of P&B collection
by Pat Sloan.

This was my first commissioned work with P&B in 2002. They really liked it, but since the pattern took four pages, they were not able to offer it as a free pattern. It is smaller than the pattern with the same name in the book since it has a 7" block. I learned a lot after making this quilt — that the fabric companies want easier quilts!

Kay's Iris Garden
By Sharon Sharp, Pekin, Illinois, 2008,
Wall size, 36" x 36" Quilted by Jane
Coons, Chesterfield, Missouri

I taught a weekend retreat of the Stars Over
St. Louis quilt at one of the local quilt guilds in
St. Louis. Being there all weekend was great
because I got to see some of the quilts almost
finished. Sharon made this quilt in memory of
a dear friend who loved Iris flowers.

Gallery

Flowering Stars

Made and quilted by Julie Brandenburg,
Montgomery City, Missouri, 2008,
Small wall size, 18" x 18"

This was another quilt that came out of the weekend workshop. Julie chose a colorful print with a dark background for the border and stars. Her kaleidoscope designs were so much fun! The coordinating orange fabric really accentuates the orange in the floral.

Stars Over St. Louis

Made and quilted by Connie Barnett,
Florissant, Mo., 2008

Small wall size, 18" x 18"

Another quilt from the same weekend workshop in
St. Louis. Connie chose a pale print for the border
and stars. Her accent fabrics bring out the orange
and turquoise in the border and stars.

Gallery

Stars Over St. Louis
Made and quilted by
Toby Lischko
Small wall size, 18" x 18",
Unfinished
Fabric courtesy of
Timeless Treasures.

I received some sample fabrics from Timeless Treasures and I wanted to see if I could create this small quilt from fat quarters. The fabric in the stars was a smaller print than the border but they were very similar prints. I was able to do it with five fat quarters. The fabric in the star points were two similar prints with different color backgrounds. I alternated the colors in the center of the St. Louis Star and on the LeMoyne Stars.

Here's to the Red, White, and Blue, Holiday Version
By Mary Nelson, Robertsville, Mo.
Wall size, 53" x 53", Unfinished
Fabric courtesy of Hoffman Fabrics.

I needed someone to test my piecing directions on the St. Louis Star and Log Cabin and Mary was nice enough to be my tester. In shades of red, green, and cream, it makes a beautiful holiday quilt. Mary said she did not have any problems following my directions and her stars came out perfect!

Gallery

Cats in Stars
By Toby Lischko,
36" x 36", Unfinished.
Fabric courtesy of
Clothworks.

I was given some Laurel Burch fabrics to work with for a quilt in *McCall's Quilting*. I had fun finding different cats in different colors for the centers of the St. Louis Star blocks. I used an attic window effect around the blocks. I want to put another border on it, but I can't decide what kind of border it needs. (I tried really hard to get it done for the book but ran out of time!)

Stars Over St. Louis

Made and quilted by Toby Lischko,
36" x 36", 2008
Fabric courtesy of Timeless Treasures.

I had this beautiful border print leftover from a
quilt project I did for Timeless Treasures. It was
irresistible to use for the fussy-cut stars. The
accent fabrics blend in well with the flowers.
It makes a fantastic fall quilt.

Templates

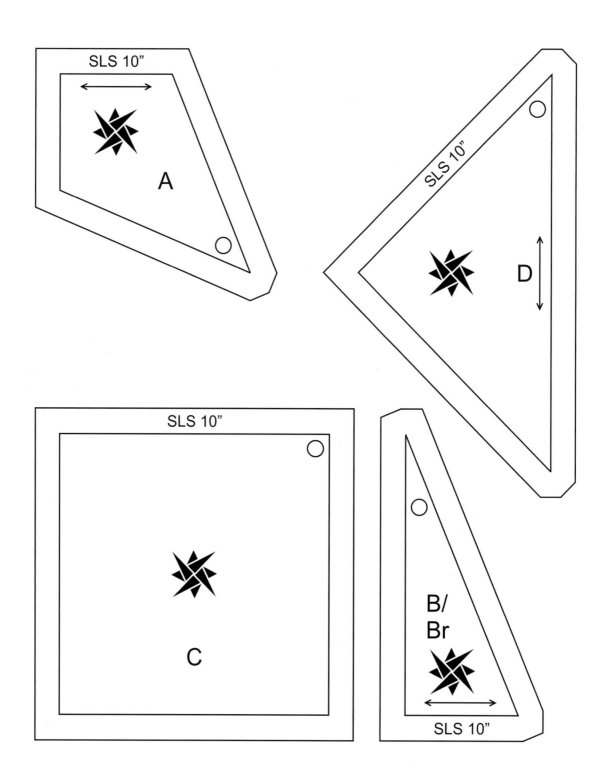

SLS 10"

A

SLS 10"

D

SLS 10"

C

B/
Br

SLS 10"

SLS 12"

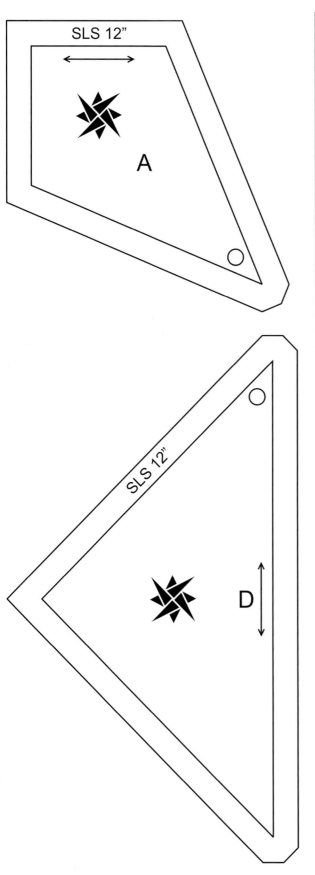

A

SLS 12"

C

SLS 12"

D

12" St. Louis Star
Reproduction Stars
Ornamental Stars
Autumn in New England
Falling Stars

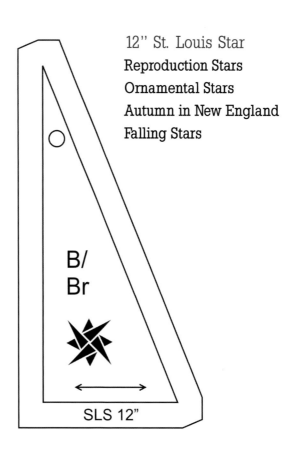

B/
Br

SLS 12"

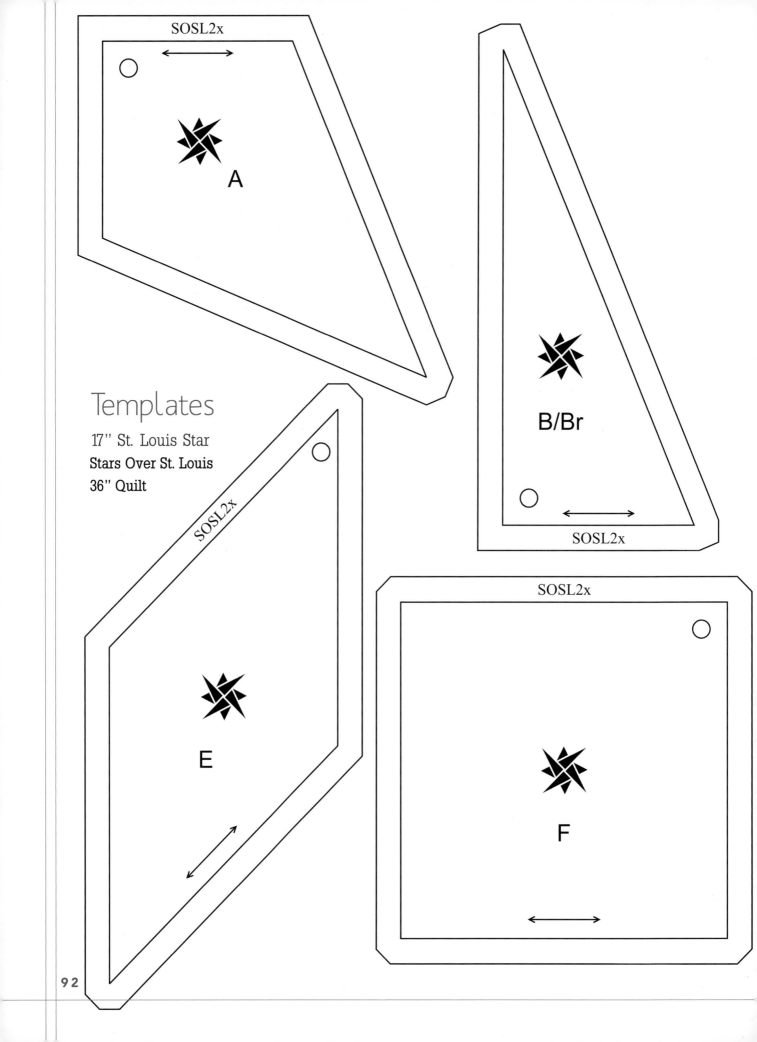

SOSL2x

A

SOSL2x

B/Br

Templates

17" St. Louis Star
Stars Over St. Louis
36" Quilt

SOSL2x

E

SOSL2x

F

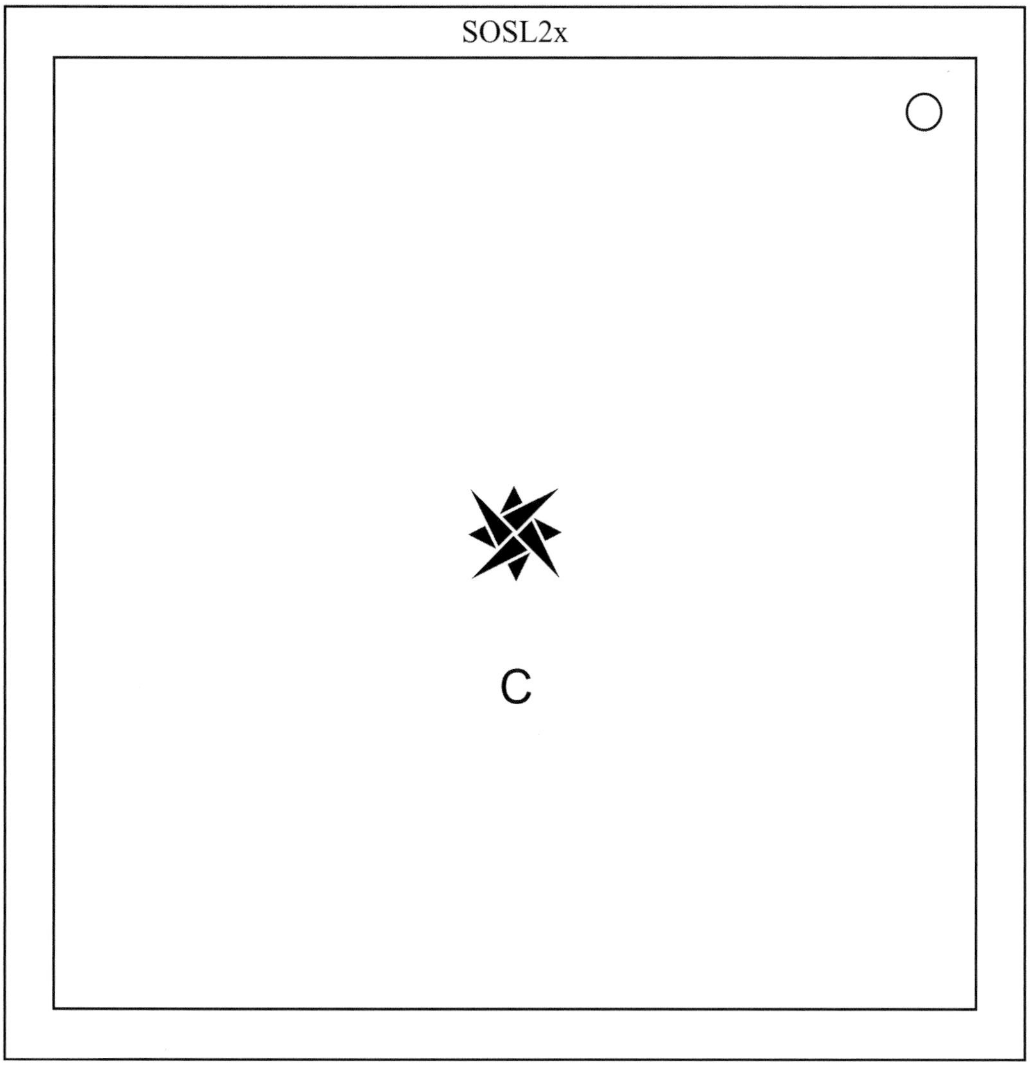

SOSL2x

C

17'' St. Louis Star
Stars Over St. Louis
36'' Quilt

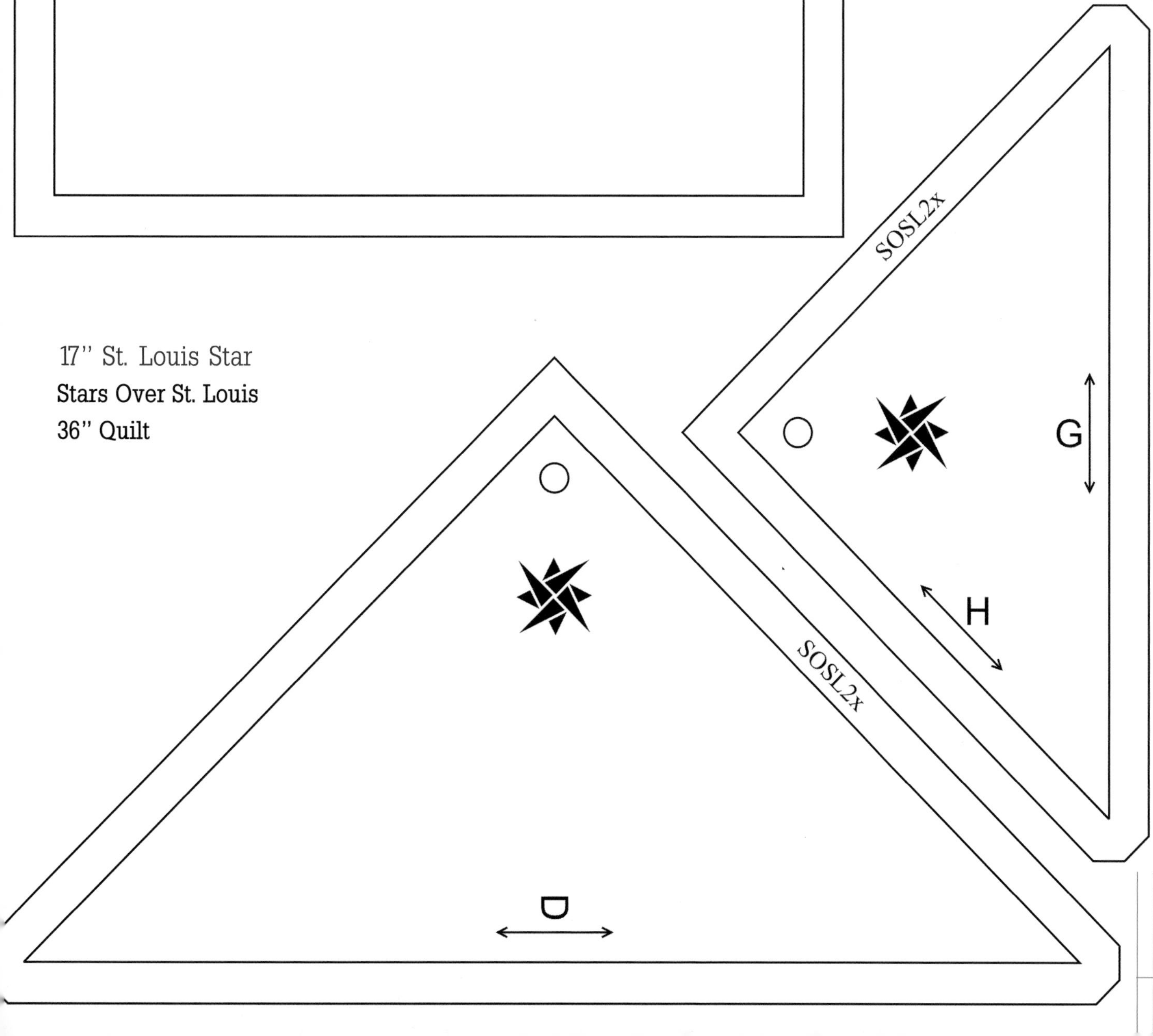

SOSL2x

G

H

SOSL2x

D

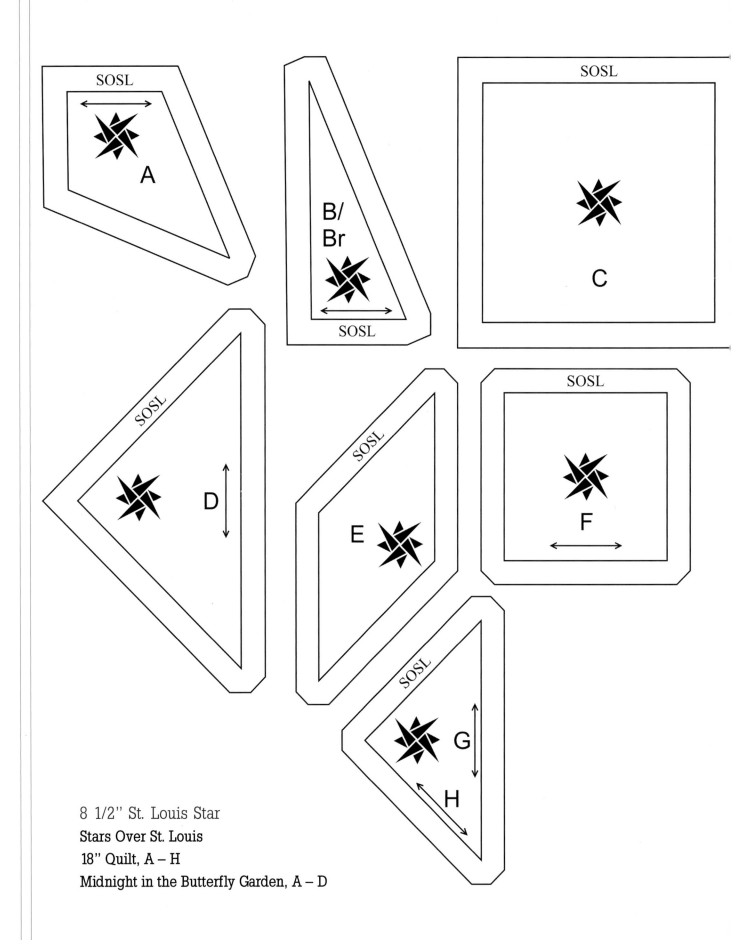

SOSL

A

B/
Br

SOSL

SOSL

C

SOSL

D

SOSL

E

SOSL

F

SOSL

G

H

8 1/2" St. Louis Star

Stars Over St. Louis

18" Quilt, A – H

Midnight in the Butterfly Garden, A – D